I0755713

Pattern Book

Christopher Russell

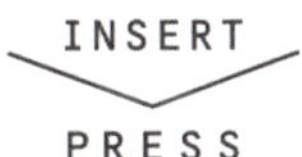

Blanc
Press
Los Angeles, California

With the exception of c[illegible] vertically, blowing a charred [illegible] sagging shingle and leaving [illegible] unscathed, it was difficult to te[illegible] been abandoned. There was a p[illegible] of disrepair or disassemble. A m[illegible] mean empty, just broken. Broken [illegible] peeling veneer revealing the skelet[illegible] core. Several families might live be[illegible] protected only by an aluminum m[illegible] entrance. Their pooled resources fe[illegible] naked children, covered a miniscule mort[illegible] against the home, that meager inheritanc[illegible] and speed don't come cheap.

Discerning decrepit from abandoned is a[illegible] of connoisseurship. After people leave, the[illegible] are the first to go. Kids don't start the destru[illegible] they finish it. Kids don't understand that a house [illegible] copper mine, and the junk of its guts gets traded [illegible] cash.

After pans and clothes are packed into the be[illegible] of an El Camino, under flashlight and moonlight, the house is open to all. The neighbors' friendly waving hands become the desperado's violent grasp: punching through plaster, pulling out wire. Wad it up, burn it up. The plastic housing melts away leaving pure salvage value in its place. Maybe 80 cents a pound.

Toilets, swag lamps, faucets and drawer pulls are currency, replacements for something broken, saved for a special occasion. Poverty is navigated with a stockpile of porcelain and pull-chains. Potential use, potential value, trash to trade in a time of need.

When kids come, windows break. It's an introduction to transgression, breaking a familial structure from a safe distance. The duration of a rock's flight through space allows plausible deniability, the warped reflection of total destruction.

Graffiti inscribes new values: loves and hates, cunts and fucks, lyrics for feelings, gypsum dust scraped into lines.

Bodies replace Barbies. Square haircuts and ink pen makeovers become the taste of tongue and sweat, the smells of crotch and jerky breath. Coke cans become beer cans, black label bottles among cigarette butts. Practicing addiction is a private affair; its public premier must be convincing. Growing up means learning tolerance, but still, no niggers allowed.

Front yards were junkyards and back yards were worse. The front yard held forgotten fruit trees, planted for sustenance by a depression era mother. Most remained small, withered. Only one was suitable for climbing. Debris piled around trees, the strewn remains of home improvement. A rusty lawnmower, poised to tackle the weeds that grew up through its wheels. A useless red wagon, leaning at one corner, its red body rinsed with rust. The metal became a jagged filigree mapping an

Discerning decrepit from abandoned is a matter of connoisseurship. After people leave, the walls are the first to go. Kids don't start the destruction; they finish it. Kids don't understand that a house is a copper mine, and the junk of its guts gets traded for cash.

After pans and clothes are packed into the bed of an El Camino, under flashlight and moonlight, the house is open to all. The neighbors' friendly waving hands become the desperado's violent grasp, punching through plaster, pulling out wire. Wad it up, burn it up. The plastic housing melts away leaving pure salvage value in its place. Maybe 80 cents a pound.

Toilets, swag lamps, faucets and drawer pulls, currency, replacements for something broken, saved for a special occasion. Poverty is navigated by a stockpile of porcelain and pull-chains, potential use, potential value, trash to trade of need.

When kids come, windows break.

Pattern Book: Christopher Russell
Insert Blanc Press February, 2013

ISBN: 978-0-9814623-7-0

Table of Contents

Essays 7

Adventures in Reading
by Holly Myers 9

The Middle of Next Week: Christopher Russell's Wallpaper Mind
by Kevin Killian 11

Patterns 15

Honeysuckle
after William Morris 16

Bird & Anenome
after William Morris 32

Peacock Feathers
after Arthur Silver 48

Trellis
after William Morris 62

Bats & Poppies
after Maurice Pillard Verneuil 74

Essays

Adventures in Reading
by Holly Myers

Given the doomsday rhetoric that tends to surround any discussion of the fate of the written word, one is inclined—indeed, one is frequently encouraged—to believe that any writer of sound mind would bend over backward to have his work read. E-books and blogs, adaptations and film rights, storylines adapted to an adolescent reading level (propped up by a surfeit of New York Times Book Review theorizing as to why the concerns of adolescence are the new universal)—most everything associated with the literary establishment today would have you believe the written word to be a floundering sell, the success of the writer contingent on the probably futile seduction of a populace terminally disinclined to care. Ease of access—whether technological, psychological, or intellectual—is everything.

Christopher Russell would beg to differ. While others strive to make reading easy, Russell goes out of his way to complicate the process. Much of his early work was composed anonymously and distributed guerilla style in restrooms, parks, and other public locales—a strategy that served to dislodge readers from the presumption-forming comforts of an authorial context. His literary art 'zine *Bedwetter*, launched in 2002, was packaged in knots of sealed envelopes and staples, such that you had to destroy each issue in order to read it. More recently, Russell weaves his writing into pictures, burying his literary self in the cloak of an art career and implicitly insisting, against the grain in both directions, on their mutual interdependency. He chops his text into geometric shapes, casts it in rainbow colors and visually assaultive fonts, and scratches it onto photographs. In the work contained here, in *Pattern Book*, he laces text into art nouveau wallpaper, dissolving his stories into a swooning screen of domestic pattern. At every turn, it seems, Russell throws some wrench into the cogs of literary consumption, slowing the reader down, jostling expectations, demanding attention—challenging the reader, in other words, to really want to be reading.

Why make it difficult? I once asked Russell over email.

"Adventure," he replied.

The brevity of his response was coy but reasonable, given the notoriously poor adaptation of his writing instrument at the time, the iPhone, to the composition of unabbreviated words (much less sentences). Several hours later, however, he sent another email: "It has to do with the current state of appreciation of the written word, which is rapidly declining, except for small, esoteric clusters of people. Writing seems to have found a comfortable niche as a feeder industry for Hollywood. The adaptation is the completion of the text in a way."

"What I'm doing is saying no to that. This is a fully formed piece that uses all the tools of design and printing to make the case for the written word as an end product, as something that is a worthy exploration. Reading these pieces slows time even more than reading already does, but that's part of the adventure."

He was still on his iPhone, writing from a parking lot—which points to another essential element: Russell is one of those compulsive, soft-spoken, internally laborious individuals who, in defiance of the iPhone and all other rhetorically debilitating contrivances of contemporary culture, genuinely cares about sentences. Plenty of visual artists use text in their work, often to clever, lyrical, even profound effect, but few can be said to be good writers. Russell is.

"The scenes of Goya are gouged and smeared at the bottom of the door. It's all smoke and limbs. Nature isn't even left standing. Just the door." "Dissolution is a feeling, and she's just a background. Everything important is engulfed in static. Her face is drawn in dark felt against the off-black space of the world. There's nothing mundane left for her to shine against." "Muddy lace panties. A stiffened brown bundle among dried yellow weeds, surrounded by foxtails and rabbit shit." "Each morning she left the constructing comfort of the forest canopy and caught the bus to Antarctica."

It may be tricky to pinpoint the who or what or when or why of Russell's sentences as they pertain to the drifting cloudscapes of his narratives, but there's no mistaking the feel for language. When he pulls a stray sentence from the body of a story and leaves it to float alone on a page or across the silvery surface of a photograph, as his does occasionally in his novel *Sniper*, even the simplest has the heft to stand alone. ("'You have blood on your shirt.' / 'So do you.'") When he keeps his sentences woven and bound together, as he does in *Pattern Book*, the effect is lush and immersive, often chillingly so. His stories drift through the darker corners of the world, through abandoned houses and tawdry liaisons and dishwasher gigs and cheap Hollywood apartments filled with smoke and the sound of pornography. His characters, to the degree that we may discern their outlines, haunt the fringes of what we're comfortable thinking about. There is a peripheral quality, a sense of watchfulness. There is a kind of longing that tips again and again between lust and generosity.

If Russell challenges us to want to be reading, the provocation is balanced by the fact that his prose is well worth reading. It is a crucial distinction. This is not difficulty for the sake of difficulty, experimentation that aims to derail the very experience of reading, but rather a taking up, a prodding, a digging into and opening out from the snug, agreeable confines of that experience. When you stand at a wall, squinting to read the tiny print hidden in the patterns of the wallpaper, there's no getting away from the sensations of reading: the movement of the eyes, head and body; the push and pull of the mind's attention; the internal battles of curiosity and fatigue. That the stories themselves seem not to have been written so much as stained, left across the walls in smudges and traces, with narratives that feel like the psychic cigarette smoke of a room's previous inhabitant, has the effect of extending the physical and cognitive challenge into the realm of the psychological. *Pattern Book*, being, of course, a book, eases up on the former to privilege the latter, but if the ratio is altered the complexity remains.

And it is complexity, not ease, Russell insists in this work, that will uphold the dignity and thus ensure the future of the precariously fated written word.

The Middle of Next Week: Christopher Russell's Wallpaper Mind

by Kevin Killian

When did wallpaper get so sinister? Some ascribe its current—and shady—reputation to the popularity that Charlotte Perkins Gilman's *The Yellow Wallpaper* achieved, after its rediscovery by second wave feminism in the 1960s and 70s. If you haven't read the story, a woman is being treated for an emotional breakdown and confined to a space with a pleasant yellow wallpaper, but gradually the reader, and the heroine, begin to suspect it is the wallpaper itself that is driving her mad. Well, the larger picture is that women are everywhere prisoners of domestic duty and limited horizons. There was also that Thurber cartoon, in which a landlady at a boarding house shows a new tenant into a room covered by a fantastically exotic and sprawling wallpaper, and the caption reads, "I think you'll like this room, Mr. Robinson. It's where my late husband Phil lost his mind." For centuries wallpaper has been the site in which anxieties about economic and cultural production have been displayed and played out on a wide scale. Oliver Cromwell and the Puritans, for example, were seriously offended by wallpaper, which they viewed as an alarming example of decadence. Stone walls were good enough for our Lord, why not for the people of England? It wasn't until Charles II was restored than one dared to paste some patterned paper to one's walls. New technologies, including steam-driven printing presses, introduced in the Regency Era, allowed middle and working class people access to affordable wallpaper for the first time, and the Victorian age became a paradise of lovably ugly papers. This period culminated in the utopian visions of William Morris and his Arts and Crafts movement, and slightly later in the Omega Workshop of the Bloomsbury circle, both movements pioneered by dreamers who imagined that even the worst slum neighborhoods could be brightened by paper designed by dedicated, socialist, often wealthy artists, and by the work of skilled laborers called paperhangers. It is not the sort of thing I would try myself, having been scarred as a youth by endless repeats of episode #43 of *I Love Lucy*, "Redecorating," in which Lucy and Ethel install a violently striped paper themselves—to save Ricky money—with diagonal results—a room so crazy that the resulting visual cues render them unable to walk without wobbling and falling. And wasn't Adolf Hitler a paperhanger? And what about that unfortunate couple whose poodle or chihuahua became a bump behind their wallpaper? I believe these stories, urban legends, stick in one's mind because they articulate fantasies about aspects of modern life that are too uncomfortable to examine closely otherwise, so they become literally the "big picture," the climate of opinion one can't even see, the forest for the trees. Now that I think of it, NYC-based designers Russel and Mary Wright, whose "American Modern" dishware and furniture fit squarely into the tradition of combining chic with populist aspiration, sort of dropped the ball in regards to wallpaper, didn't they? They designed a few rolls and patterns, but their hearts weren't in it, not really. They were Cromwellians at heart perhaps.

Now when we think of wallpaper we are most likely to think first of its virtual version. I'm writing this right now at my office, where a "wallpaper" of a bright farmscape (like *Christina's World* with a happy Frank Capra glow) lurks around the edges of the blank page—who named that effect "wallpaper"? Dodie told me once that computer scientists had to have wallpaper, otherwise the screen would freeze and crack open and all the pixel dust would seep out—don't know how true that is, but again, it illustrates the social safeguarding we feel a good, or even a bad, wallpaper brings to our fragile domestic lives. We need something to keep out the pixel dust.

In San Francisco in the early 1980s, Bruce Boone had a huge crush on Stephen King and his novels, which fascinated and repelled him at the same time on a stylistic level. His books are so long, Bruce finally decided, because they are basically *wallpaper writing*, page after page not of beautiful writing in the accepted sense, but of efficient writing, that sort one needs to set up a scene, or the scene itself. Our contemporary, poet Carla Harryman, speaks to the same point in a recent interview (with Renee Gladman, in the online journal *How 2*), as she discusses her attraction to Kathy Acker's writing. "I was interested in Acker's use of repetition and redundancy as a mode of filling up negative, self-canceling space with noise, which would also result in an edgy idea or prose-work as conceptual object." The need to fill up negative, self-cancelling space has surely led to some behemoth projects; is the self-cancellation then negated or defeated, made a positive space again? Millions of Stephen King fans would agree, at least they used to, before King's late career turn to just not giving a shit.

I was born wanting a Christopher Russell to join me in this confusing world.... I wanted a boy with confused gaze, mortified as I am by the harsh and ugly crumples of life, but one who, with bold decisive strokes, could hack a pathway out if it. And finally, one day, I overheard two friends talking about an artist called "Christopher Russell." Such a beautiful name, a dreamy faced blond boy like Christopher Robin, but with that "rustle" connotation; language spoken softly, the ways the leaves speak it. These friends spoke of him as an artist with a camera, an artist who, while still a schoolboy, had documented the radical world of public sex in San Francisco. Yeah man, he like, hid his camera in his crotch, and he'd unzip his fly like you would if you were having sex, and the camera snapped a picture of whatever its lens saw. Somehow I acquired one of these photos and it has sat surveying my living room for years now, a moment of black and white sexual possession, like a still from a Andrzej Żuławski film.

I wondered what Russell thought of the relation between text and image. I was so into figurative work that people would come to my place—art type people—look at the work hanging on the walls, and they were all like, there are words in every piece! Dismissively, as though this foible proved beyond the shadow of a doubt that I was a poet, and that a poet couldn't do otherwise than admire work by Joe Brainard, Chris Johanson, Sue Coe, Raymond Pettibon, Lutz Bacher. Julian Myers was plain exasperated, for I was using words as crutches, unable perhaps to face the truth of the image, or the gesture, without words to explain it or take its sting away. We had some spirited discussions, and Lord knows I've been haughty when I see movie posters framed in people's apartments or homes. Russell was a prose writer, a fiction writer, it developed, and furthermore had a way queer zine called *Bedwetter*. I sent him a story to publish, for his calendar issue—the conceit was that you could hang the issue on your wall as a calendar, each page had a different look but roughly represented a month. I forget what month I was, but I did notice that when you opened to my story, you were looking at something that no longer looked like text; and I connected this to the wallpaper writing of which Bruce spoke, in which text could be used as a purely gestural way, so it's no coincidence really that the present volume is the product of the robustly conceptual Insert Blanc Press. We were at a Chinese restaurant once and I nearly proposed to Russell that we could do a story based entirely on the fortunes inside fortune cookies. I kept my mouth shut, remembering a similar scene in Stephen King's *It*, where the band of beleaguered heroes go to a Chinese restaurant to escape from the clown Pennywhistle, and when they break open their fortune cookies, awful things lie within—an eyeball—a baby frog—worms. It made me shriek when *It* first came out. Then I got a fortune last week that reads, "Three months from today something great will happen to you." I suppose by the time this book comes out my great day will have come and gone—you can call me to find out what it was that happened to me. Sorry for the smear of tenses, but I was trying, like any other prediction, to enjamb past, present and future into one.

Russell's method, in which he dethrones language's hegemony over rival visual formations by distorting and exaggerating its recognizable, even homey, patterns borrows roots from many traditions. Medieval monks are said to have curried favor with abbots by carving Bible verses into the head of a pin. A sharp monocle was fetched, applied to the abbot's eye, he squinted and lo, in front of him appeared the opening words of Genesis. But cast away the glass and the words went away, back into the camouflage of the utile. What was that famous painting of two noble Dutch lords, proud and serious, but if you stood under it all the way to the left, and cast your gaze sideways, a skull popped out at you? Otherwise you saw a smear, like the men are floating in a throw rug made of potholder string vomit. Hans Holbein's "The Ambassadors" from 1533.

When language, or the image, is enervated, the work of art has room for other connotations to manifest. Oh! Those hidden pictures in *Highlights*, the magazine for children! Find the milk bottle in the tiger's fur. Lewis Carroll's parodies and pastiches destabilizing high Victorian certainty, such as "The Mad Gardener's Song," from *Sylvie and Bruno* (1889):

> He thought he saw a Buffalo
> Upon the chimney-piece:
> He looked again, and found it was
> His Sister's Husband's Niece.
> "Unless you leave this house," he said,
> "I'll send for the police!"
>
> He thought he saw a Rattlesnake
> That questioned him in Greek:
> He looked again, and found it was
> The Middle of Next Week.
> "The one thing I regret," he said,
> "Is that it cannot speak!"
>
> He thought he saw a Banker's Clerk
> Descending from the bus:
> He looked again, and found it was
> A Hippopotamus.
> "If this should stay to dine," he said,
> "There won't be much for us!"

Or how when I was a boy, I ran to the store to buy the Sunday New York Times, to find out how many times what's his name had hidden the name of his daughter in the hair of Julie Andrews or Robert Preston, or the befurled gowns of Carol Channing? Hirschfeld! Nina! I thought of how Nina would be pleased at first, but after fifty years of this wasn't she tired of Dad's obsession with her name, start to wish he had called her something a little more difficult to double as fringe? Something like "Brooke"? Then a chilling thought followed her first, had father foreseen what he would do even at the baptismal font, when he said, Let's call her Nina? Because it would be a name easy enough to foreground? Hirschfeld left a number by his logo slash signature, right? It would say Hirschfeld 4, so an insider would look for the word Nina four times. A little later on, as a teen, I believed that the stars on each issue of Playboy, inside the letter P, represented the number of times Hefner had fucked the model in that month's centerfold. Other boys thought that if there were four stars, it just meant that she was great, not that they had had sex four times. If the stars appeared outside of the "P," which sometimes happened, it was that she had resisted his best efforts. You had to root for those girls, if you ask me. Even at four I was a feminist; and around this time psychedelic drugs started warping the traditional Palmer method of handwriting. In San Francisco, where I live now, a cadre of poster artists challenged you to figure out what event was being promoted by manipulating alphabetical characters and numerals in monstrous, wonderful ways. The famous drawing on the cover of the Grateful Dead's "American Beauty" album, some of us deadheads swore it read American Reality. It was the unsettling, duck-rabbit paradox of Wittgenstein.

It meant something, it was a diagnosis, of what sort of person you are, how much, and what, you might read into any given image. Rorschach made a fortune that way. The ink was applied, the paper folded over, and when you opened the paper again, you saw a turkey spread its wings or you saw your mother's vagina and your face deep within it looking scared to death and afraid to emerge. And in these beautiful pages we will see, and we will not see, things it will take us a hundred years to understand.

Patterns

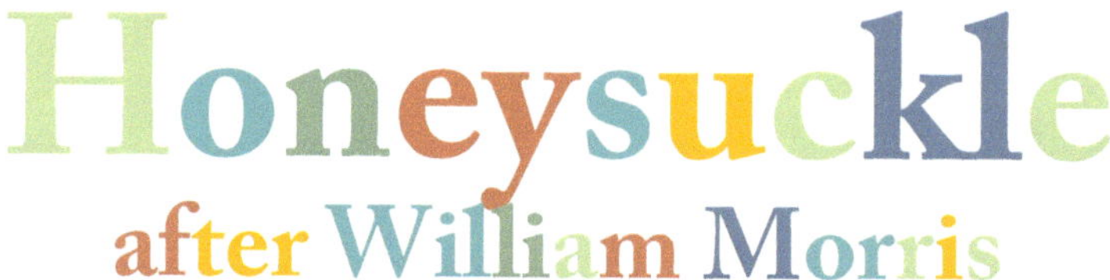
Honeysuckle
after William Morris

Part One: I didn't mind institutional life. I got three meals. Food was always hot and on time. I never had to cook or even wash a dish. I even just pretended to wash my hands. I didn't use soap, so there were still millions of invisible germs making highways of my fingerprints. I like myself that way. I wasn't filthy, because I seemed clean. Nobody could imagine the diseases latent on my fingertips. Secrets feel close to home, they're all I know.

I didn't have to do laundry. I had to make my bed, but faked it. I didn't let myself toss. I slept still; the sheets couldn't come untucked. I had to suppress my dreams to maintain a faint awareness of my body. I had to override the irrational movements that came out of dreaming. I didn't know the procedure for folding sheets around a mattress. I could have asked anybody, but that would have given up too much of myself. If the nurses saw a single limit, they could begin to define me. If I delivered an impression of maturity and intelligent grace, they wouldn't piece me into something else. Their manipulations would begin at the first unrefined edge.

Bedtime began flat on my back, arms folded across my chest, but I couldn't stay that way for long. I felt the a flutter from levitation, and a dull sense of loss. I couldn't stop it. I tried, panicked eyes and stiff throat. I could only look down on myself, at those arms crossed over my chest. I'd assumed the posture of a vampire sleeping in his coffin. I was posed as the prince of darkness, yet I didn't feel safe. A word for a monster, power and evil, it was in my head, in my room. It just scared me. I knew what I'd seen from above, so I gave up. I put my hands on my pillow. I felt the sinking in my head instead of my stomach. The vampire spell was broken.

I wouldn't make another move until I folded the blankets off of me in the morning. When I stretched the wrinkles out of the sheets, there was always a little extra. I'd leave the unnecessary fabric deeply wrinkled, smashed flush with the mattress. I'd cover the excess with the slightly fuzzy, baby blue, polyester hospital blanket. It was that color that could trick anyone into feeling at home now and then.

By the time I was through, there wasn't a visible wrinkle. Nobody could have known my inexperience with hospital corners. On inspection, I got the praise I needed.

They trusted me. My good natured obedience and unassuming smile were as fake as the Wellbutrin induced contentment dispensed at regular intervals from the medicine window. My shyness, rather my silence, won their trust. With youth, quietness is the most revered quality. Later in life, reserve signifies something sinister. But the nurses ran with common sense assumptions and never checked the details. I stayed hidden. They didn't know that through all of my docile nodding, I kept notes. I scanned for stray sounds that might refine my larger sense of the institution. Every new word was processed against all the other information I gathered. I'd eventually turn their words to my own purposes, use the rules of the hospital to effect an efficient escape.

Good behavior would eventually get me outside the building. There was a system of points that would win me 15 minutes outside, unsupervised. I'd have to be ready when it came; it's not a lot of time. I didn't mind the institution, but I had another life on the outside that carried on despite my absence. It would make contact in little bursts like the previews to a movie, though quicker and entirely visceral, a cramp, or a sigh. If I weren't simultaneously on the trail and on the run, if danger were to pass, I could stay forever in regimented paradise.

My doctor was a pretty average guy. He paid his dues, and paid his bills. He didn't seem like the type to push beyond a good book, comfortable chair and regular contributions to PBS. He wasn't caught up in some quest for a trophy blond, and didn't know the vocabulary of the track. I don't know why he got involved with them. Maybe evil was just his response to boredom. Everybody needs a hobby. He tried to win me over and take my confidence as his prize. But I knew too much. I knew his employer, not by name, but by crime.

I couldn't say what I knew. Every session I performed the role of bored, depressed teenager evading a discussion of consuming and confusing feelings. I was desperate to tell my story. But I couldn't finish. I didn't know how they found me out. It should have been different. Maybe it was a spy in my own head who replaced the cyanide tablets with Pez.

The doctor always wanted to know what I knew. I had to swallow. I couldn't give him enough to assess my threat. "So how are you feeling today?" "I miss TV." "Can we talk about what brought you here?" "An ambulance. I remember the paramedic. She was a woman with curly brown hair, a plain gold cross on a thin chain, pink turtleneck under her uniform and I noticed a chipped nail, burgundy. But I don't remember her name. I was dying, her name wouldn't have done any good." "Do you think you were dying?" "I don't know. I guess. No." "You told somebody you'd swallowed cyanide, but you hadn't. We call that a cry for help. What brought you to that point; what can I help you with?" "It's just something I saw on TV. Batman or something. The Penguin, I don't know." "Do you like super heros?" "No. I just watch whatever's on, except news. I'll watch anything, it's all the same, something to fill my head, pass the time". "Eventually, you'll tell me". I filtered through his casually optimistic facade for the intentions that lingered beneath his breath.

Once I asked what he wrote in his pad. I looked down, diverted my eyes to the side. With a nervously aspirated squeak, I made my request. He wasn't convinced. "I'm just keeping notes of your progress". But he received the image of innocence and inadequacy. Through repeated exposure he'll believe.

It didn't matter. I knew what he'd written. I could hear the sounds. They crossed the room like a dissipating trail of smoke. With careful concentration, I could catch the nuances of pen scratching against paper. I knew how to build the sounds into the letter forms that would combine into the doctor's words in my head.

I needed to tell the story, that linoleum. It's grid of squares, each marked by an ochre snowflake against an orange pattern with its sketchy geometric impression of sunburst or sunshine. It was covered by a million tiny, shimmering drops, some sort of liquid Vegas spread thin across the floor. They tried to clean up. They couldn't have known I was coming. Anybody would have assumed it was a freshly cleaned floor. But sloshed into the corner were the tiny coagulated chunks and a few red drops that shifted and merged with residual wash water.

I had to get out. The adolescent ward wore me down. I learned to live inside my head, but I struggled against that stupid need for human interaction. I woke up one morning saying "I love you!" I stood, fully awake, and hugged an armload of air. I pressed it gently with my tongue. My lips closed, holding everything inside.

Part 2: His story begins along a secluded street wedged between a freeway off ramp and a neglected city park. The houses emerged as the typically uniform post war construction that delivered the sense of confinement a GI would call home. Over time, places were bought and sold, each new occupant added to the aesthetic until regiment was lost to traces of eccentric whims. Examining the architecture was like past life regression. The Mediterranean chandelier that hung over green shag carpet alongside colonial oak paneling with an Empire lamp stand next to the lazy boy.

The seclusion of the small tract allowed the residents a certain liberty in constructing their private versions of paradise. Wayne's neighbors had peacocks that flew up to the rooftop to serenade each other with the tortured falsettos of battered children. The yard was dominated by a weeping willow, and despite regular droughts, always seemed to be cool and muddy. The gate to Wayne's picket fence was flanked by Napoleonic lions that guarded the cement bestiary whose residents dwarfed the delicately painted virgin Mary they'd been placed to adore. (Wayne's parents weren't Catholic, but they didn't want to live with the guilt of destroying religious art). The life sized deer became a stationary carousel from which Wayne saw the world by cocking his head.

The actual home was a reconstructed as a miniature stucco plantation house. Despite Wayne's room full of curiosities, each designed to socialize children to the arts and sciences, he hated being inside. He wanted nothing more than to cross the street and wander the dusty trails, among the tall oaks, dying grasses, racing squirrels, trickling creek and discarded exoskeletons. There were so many nooks to pursue. Among the trees, Wayne was expected to tune out the world and enter completely into the constructions of his mind.

His mother preferred the edge of the park, where a small section was leveled and green. In his mother's park, the trees weren't placed for natural occlusion, but to provide shade to the picnic tables and swing set. Wayne found retreat in the lulling motion of the swing. Even nauseous, he'd persist in swinging as high as he could. He liked to watch the world from the swing mistaking angles for perspectives.

A constantly changing row of cars always lined the street. From varying heights he would watch the men that sat in their cars, waiting for a pedestrian to take the passenger seat. Some times the men would emerge from their cars and enter the rough shrubs and poison oak.

Knowing that strangers don't talk to each other, he determined that the men in the cars were engaged in the surreptitious dealings that filtered off the TV and out into the world through his mind. He heard their discussions of stolen gold, counterfeit bills and other sorts of booty. The feeble old man with liver spotted hands, whose turtleneck looked like a fresh wash of hanging skin seemed to be the king of them all. Despite his reluctant spine, he was always at the park, and spoke to everybody. He had a big and bright smile. The firmness of his lips seemed out of place between jowls.

Wayne focused on his golden medallion. He dreamed of toppling the old man and grabbing it for himself. Other men offered less temptation, only signet rings and dusty loafers. It was all right to dream of plunder. As a crook, the old man's gold was stolen from thieves to be stolen again.

Part Three: Laws will still govern my body after I die. There's no loitering. There's that offensive smell, and my complexion might be troubling. Alleyways are no longer an option.

I wouldn't mind someplace remote, an unresolved territory where children and vagrants find themselves. A chance encounter with a corpse satisfies one childhood fascination at the risk of creating another.

It would be an imposition to ask the favor of sizing me to fit Hefty bags.

Burial at sea lacks the beauty its name suggests. It's about ashes. It's not the slosh of water into the boat as my flaccid vessel is rolled overboard by fishermen in tattered yellow overalls and matching hats. My body would never have the chance to float awkwardly until, waterlogged and salted, I found a definite direction.

I guess somebody has to ask why, as if I should know the answer. I have to guess, but I suppose it's because I'm stupid. I know just enough to feel discomfort, but not enough to improve my circumstance. I only see problems, and that's a hell of a way to live. There's no wonder. Early infatuations with textbook Greece or China are as distant as ever, so I think maybe I have seen it all. I'm hungry for something beyond the rush of hyperventilation and the sublime feeling of allergy headaches. When I take a deep breath, I just don't feel anything new.

Part Four: The tinny ring of a distant radio drew Wayne to the window. He saw fire: candlelight or something fierce. The image filtered through the forest, so it was hard to tell. He saw the silhouetted breasts of ecstatic women flinging their bodies with cartoon limberness to the satanic din of an AM radio.

He changed his mind. The women were in long black robes with thick gold piping around the hoods, pacing crestfallen around the stone pit. He heard their call dodging in and out of Cool Clear Waters. Their voices came through Hank Williams like tiny scraps of paper on the floor.

He focused beyond the sound of his window. The corroded aluminum rattled along its track. The whirling laughter of the cicadas and the deeply drawn comments of the frogs added a viscosity to the air. Though it was an impression of a voice that traveled like a secret code within the sound of the radio that lured him onto the lawn.

Escape didn't require a second thought. The thrill had worn away. The world of mosquitoes, rats and playing opossum is where he felt safe. Wayne found a strange comfort in red eyes and buzzing.

Jumping out his window used to deliver a shock. But now, feeling only came with the impact of feet smashing dark footprints into a green field of tiny pearls. The suction of mud around his toes might also be enough. Thoughts of warmth, bed sheets and slippers, flashed so rapidly through his head, they became foreign.

It made sense that Wayne would experience the world while his parents slept. He never understood family the way he was supposed to. His discontent was greatest at night, when he had to focus his mind and put it to rest. Instead, he would wander, looking for clues that could be fastened together for a sense of understanding. He became sidetracked by the spectacle of nature in the pleasure of his abandonment.

That night, he avoided the thick gray mists along the creek and stuck to the sidewalk. The crackle of the radio led him three doors down. Wayne walked to the side, fascinated by the stucco monolith disrupted by a faintly glowing window. The light defined a subtle path between the house and a row of cypress trees that was almost lost in the grainy image created by the strain of rods and cones. He stared at the wall feeling what was inside. X-ray power was more premonitory than visual. A sense of purpose washed over him like a sweaty chill. He felt at ease.

He saw eyelids resting in the dull glow of the candlelight. Her skin had the slight translucency of butterscotch candy. Thin veins appeared as fragments, hiding just under the surface. Her heart was buried too deep to notice the beating, and the lungs were defined by a residue of incense smoke. Her chest didn't seem to rise or fall, and even under the warmth of the candle, she looked a little blue. Her breasts were tipped with large blots that seemed to absorb the color of the light. It reminded him of the color of scabs, sucked off his arm and held to the sun. He wondered if she tasted the same.

paneling with an Empire lamp stand next to the lazy boy.

The seclusion of the small tract allowed the residents a certain liberty in constructing their private versions of paradise. Wayne's neighbors had peacocks that flew up to the rooftop to serenade each other with the tortured falsettos of battered children. The yard was dominated by a weeping willow, and despite regular droughts, always seemed to be cool and muddy. The gate to Wayne's picket fence was flanked by Napoleonic lions that guarded the cement bestiary whose residents dwarfed the delicately painted virgin Mary they'd been placed to adore. (Wayne's parents weren't Catholic, but they didn't want to live with the guilt of destroying religious art). The life sized deer became a stationary carousel from which Wayne saw the world by cocking his head.

The actual home was a reconstructed as a miniature stucco plantation house. Despite Wayne's room full of curiosities, each designed to socialize children to the arts and sciences, he hated being inside. He wanted nothing more than to cross the street and wander the dusty trails, among the tall oaks, dying grasses, racing squirrels, trickling creek and discarded exoskeletons. There were so many nooks to pursue. Among the trees, Wayne was expected to tune out the world and enter completely into the constructions of his mind.

His mother preferred the edge of the park, where a small section was leveled and green. In his mother's park, the trees weren't placed for natural occlusion, but to provide shade to the picnic tables and swing set. Wayne found retreat in the lulling motion of the swing. Even nauseous, he'd persist in swinging as high as he could. He liked to watch the world from the swing mistaking angles for perspectives.

A constantly changing row of cars always lined the street. From varying heights he would watch the men that sat in their cars, waiting for a pedestrian to take the passenger seat. Some times the men would emerge from their cars and enter the rough shrubs and poison oak.

Knowing that strangers don't talk to each other, he determined that the men in the cars were engaged in the surreptitious dealings that filtered off the TV and out into the world through his mind. He heard their discussions of stolen gold, counterfeit bills and other sorts of booty. The feeble old man with liver spotted hands, whose turtleneck looked like a fresh wash of hanging skin seemed to be the king of them all. Despite his reluctant spine, he was always at the park, and spoke to everybody. He had a big and bright smile. The firmness of his lips seemed out of place between jowls.

Wayne focused on his golden medallion. He dreamed of toppling the old man and grabbing it for himself. Other men offered less temptation, only signet rings and dusty loafers. It was all right to dream of plunder. As a crook, the old man's gold was stolen from thieves to be stolen again.

Part Three: Laws will still govern my body after I die. There's no loitering. There's that offensive smell, and my complexion might be troubling. Alleyways are no longer an option.

I wouldn't mind someplace remote, an unresolved territory where children and vagrants find themselves. A chance encounter with a corpse satisfies one childhood fascination at the risk of creating another.

It would be an imposition to ask the favor of sizing me to fit Hefty bags.

Burial at sea lacks the beauty its name suggests. It's about ashes. It's not the slosh of water into the boat as my flaccid vessel is rolled overboard by fishermen in tattered yellow overalls and matching hats. My body would never have the chance to float awkwardly until, waterlogged and salted, I found a definite direction.

I guess somebody has to ask why, as if I should know the answer. I have to guess, but I suppose it's because I'm stupid. I know just enough to feel discomfort, but not enough to improve my circumstance. I only see problems, and that's a hell of a way to live. There's no wonder. Early infatuations with textbook Greece or China are as distant as ever, so I think maybe I have seen it all. I'm hungry for something beyond the rush of hyperventilation and the sublime feeling of allergy headaches. When I take a deep breath, I just don't feel anything new.

Part Four: The tinny ring of a distant radio drew Wayne to the window. He saw fire: candlelight or something fierce. The image filtered through the forest, so it was hard to tell. He saw the silhouetted breasts of ecstatic women flinging their bodies with cartoon limberness to the satanic din of an AM radio.

He changed his mind. The women were in long black robes with thick gold piping around the hoods, pacing crestfallen around the stone pit. He heard their call dodging in and out of Cool Clear Waters. Their voices came through Hank Williams like tiny scraps of paper on the floor.

He focused beyond the sound of his window. The corroded aluminum rattled along its track. The whirling laughter of the cicadas and the deeply drawn comments of the frogs added a viscosity to the air. Though it was an impression of a voice that traveled like a secret code within the sound of the radio that lured him onto the lawn.

Escape didn't require a second thought. The thrill had worn away. The world of mosquitoes, rats and playing opossum is where he felt safe. Wayne found a strange comfort in red eyes and buzzing.

Jumping out his window used to deliver a shock. But now, feeling only came with the impact of feet smashing dark footprints into a green field of tiny pearls. The suction of mud around his toes might also be enough. Thoughts of warmth, bed sheets and slippers, flashed so rapidly through his head, they became foreign.

It made sense that Wayne would experience the world while his parents slept. He never understood family the way he was supposed to. His discontent was greatest at night, when he had to focus his mind and put it to rest. Instead, he would wander, looking for clues that could be fastened together for a sense of understanding. He became sidetracked by the spectacle of nature in the pleasure of his abandonment.

That night, he avoided the thick gray mists along the creek and stuck to the sidewalk. The crackle of the radio led him three doors down. Wayne walked to the side, fascinated by the stucco monolith disrupted by a faintly glowing window. The light defined a subtle path between the house and a row of cypress trees that was almost lost in the grainy image created by the strain of rods and cones. He stared at the wall feeling what was inside. X-ray power was more premonitory than visual. A sense of purpose washed over him like a sweaty chill. He felt at ease.

He saw eyelids resting in the dull glow of the candlelight. Her skin had the slight translucency of butterscotch candy. Thin veins appeared as fragments, hiding just under the surface. Her heart was buried too deep to notice the beating, and the lungs were defined by a residue of incense smoke. Her chest didn't seem to rise or fall, and even under the warmth of the candle, she looked a little blue. Her breasts were tipped with large blots that seemed to absorb the color of the light. It reminded him of the color of scabs, sucked off his arm and held to the sun. He wondered if she tasted the same.

Part One: I didn't mind institutional life. I got three meals. Food was always hot and on time. I never had to cook or even wash a dish. I even just pretended to wash my hands. I didn't use soap, so there were still millions of invisible germs making highways of my fingerprints. I like myself that way. I wasn't filthy, because I seemed clean. Nobody could imagine the diseases latent on my fingertips. Secrets feel close to home, they're all I know.

I didn't have to do laundry. I had to make my bed, but faked it. I didn't let myself toss. I slept still; the sheets couldn't come untucked. I had to suppress my dreams to maintain a faint awareness of my body. I had to override the irrational movements that came out of dreaming. I didn't know the procedure for folding sheets around a mattress. I could have asked anybody, but that would have given up too much of myself. If the nurses saw a single limit, they could begin to define me. If I delivered an impression of maturity and intelligent grace, they wouldn't piece me into something else. Their manipulations would begin at the first unrefined edge.

Bedtime began flat on my back, arms folded across my chest, but I couldn't stay that way for long. I felt the a flutter from levitation, and a dull sense of loss. I couldn't stop it. I tried, panicked eyes and stiff throat. I could only look down on myself, at those arms crossed over my chest. I'd assumed the posture of a vampire sleeping in his coffin. I was posed as the prince of darkness, yet I didn't feel safe. A word for a monster, power and evil, it was in my head, in my room. It just scared me. I knew what I'd seen from above, so I gave up. I put my hands on my pillow. I felt the sinking in my head instead of my stomach. The vampire spell was broken.

I wouldn't make another move until I folded the blankets off of me in the morning. When I stretched the wrinkles out of the sheets, there was always a little extra. I'd leave the unnecessary fabric deeply wrinkled, smashed flush with the mattress. I'd cover the excess with the slightly fuzzy, baby blue, polyester hospital blanket. It was that color that could trick anyone into feeling at home now and then.

By the time I was through, there wasn't a visible wrinkle. Nobody could have known my inexperience with hospital corners. On inspection, I got the praise I needed.

They trusted me. My good natured obedience and unassuming smile were as fake as the Wellbutrin induced contentment dispensed at regular intervals from the medicine window. My shyness, rather my silence, won their trust. With youth, quietness is the most revered quality. Later in life, reserve signifies something sinister. But the nurses ran with common sense assumptions and never checked the details. I stayed hidden. They didn't know that through all of my docile nodding, I kept notes. I scanned for stray sounds that might refine my larger sense of the institution. Every new word was processed against all the other information I gathered. I'd eventually turn their words to my own purposes, use the rules of the hospital to effect an efficient escape.

Good behavior would eventually get me outside the building. There was a system of points that would win me 15 minutes outside, unsupervised. I'd have to be ready when it came; it's not a lot of time. I didn't mind the institution, but I had another life on the outside that carried on despite my absence. It would make contact in little bursts like the previews to a movie, though quicker and entirely visceral, a cramp, or a sigh. If I weren't simultaneously on the trail and on the run, if danger were to pass, I could stay forever in regimented paradise.

My doctor was a pretty average guy. He paid his dues, and paid his bills. He didn't seem like the type to push beyond a good book, comfortable chair and regular contributions to PBS. He wasn't caught up in some quest for a trophy blond, and didn't know the vocabulary of the track. I don't know why he got involved with them. Maybe evil was just his response to boredom. Everybody needs a hobby. He tried to win me over and take my confidence as his prize. But I knew too much. I knew his employer, not by name, but by crime.

I couldn't say what I knew. Every session I performed the role of bored, depressed teenager evading a discussion of consuming and confusing feelings. I was desperate to tell my story. But I couldn't finish. I didn't know how they found me out. It should have been different. Maybe it was a spy in my own head who replaced the cyanide tablets with Pez.

The doctor always wanted to know what I knew. I had to swallow. I couldn't give him enough to assess my threat. "So how are you feeling today?" "I miss TV." "Can we talk about what brought you here?" "An ambulance. I remember the paramedic. She was a woman with curly brown hair, a plain gold cross on a thin chain, pink turtleneck under her uniform and I noticed a chipped nail, burgundy. But I don't remember her name. I was dying, her name wouldn't have done any good." "Do you think you were dying?" "I don't know. I guess. No." "You told somebody you'd swallowed cyanide, but you hadn't. We call that a cry for help. What brought you to that point; what can I help you with?" "It's just something I saw on TV. Batman or something. The Penguin, I don't know." "Do you like super heros?" "No. I just watch whatever's on, except news. I'll watch anything, it's all the same, something to fill my head, pass the time". "Eventually, you'll tell me". I filtered through his casually optimistic facade for the intentions that lingered beneath his breath.

Once I asked what he wrote in his pad. I looked down, diverted my eyes to the side. With a nervously aspirated squeak, I made my request. He wasn't convinced. "I'm just keeping notes of your progress". But he received the image of innocence and inadequacy. Through repeated exposure he'll believe.

It didn't matter. I knew what he'd written. I could hear the sounds. They crossed the room like a dissipating trail of smoke. With careful concentration, I could catch the nuances of pen scratching against paper. I knew how to build the sounds into the letter forms that would combine into the doctor's words in my head.

I needed to tell the story, that linoleum. It's grid of squares, each marked by an ochre snowflake against an orange pattern with its sketchy geometric impression of sunburst or sunshine. It was covered by a million tiny, shimmering drops, some sort of liquid Vegas spread thin across the floor. They tried to clean up. They couldn't have known I was coming. Anybody would have assumed it was a freshly cleaned floor. But sloshed into the corner were the tiny coagulated chunks and a few red drops that shifted and merged with residual wash water.

I had to get out. The adolescent ward wore me down. I learned to live inside my head, but I struggled against that stupid need for human interaction. I woke up one morning saying "I love you!" I stood, fully awake, and hugged an armload of air. I pressed it gently with my tongue. My lips closed, holding everything inside.

Part 2: His story begins along a secluded street wedged between a freeway off ramp and a neglected city park. The houses emerged as the typically uniform post war construction that delivered the sense of confinement a GI would call home. Over time, places were bought and sold, each new occupant added to the aesthetic until regiment was lost to traces of eccentric whims. Examining the architecture was like past life regression. The Mediterranean chandelier that hung over green shag carpet alongside colonial oak

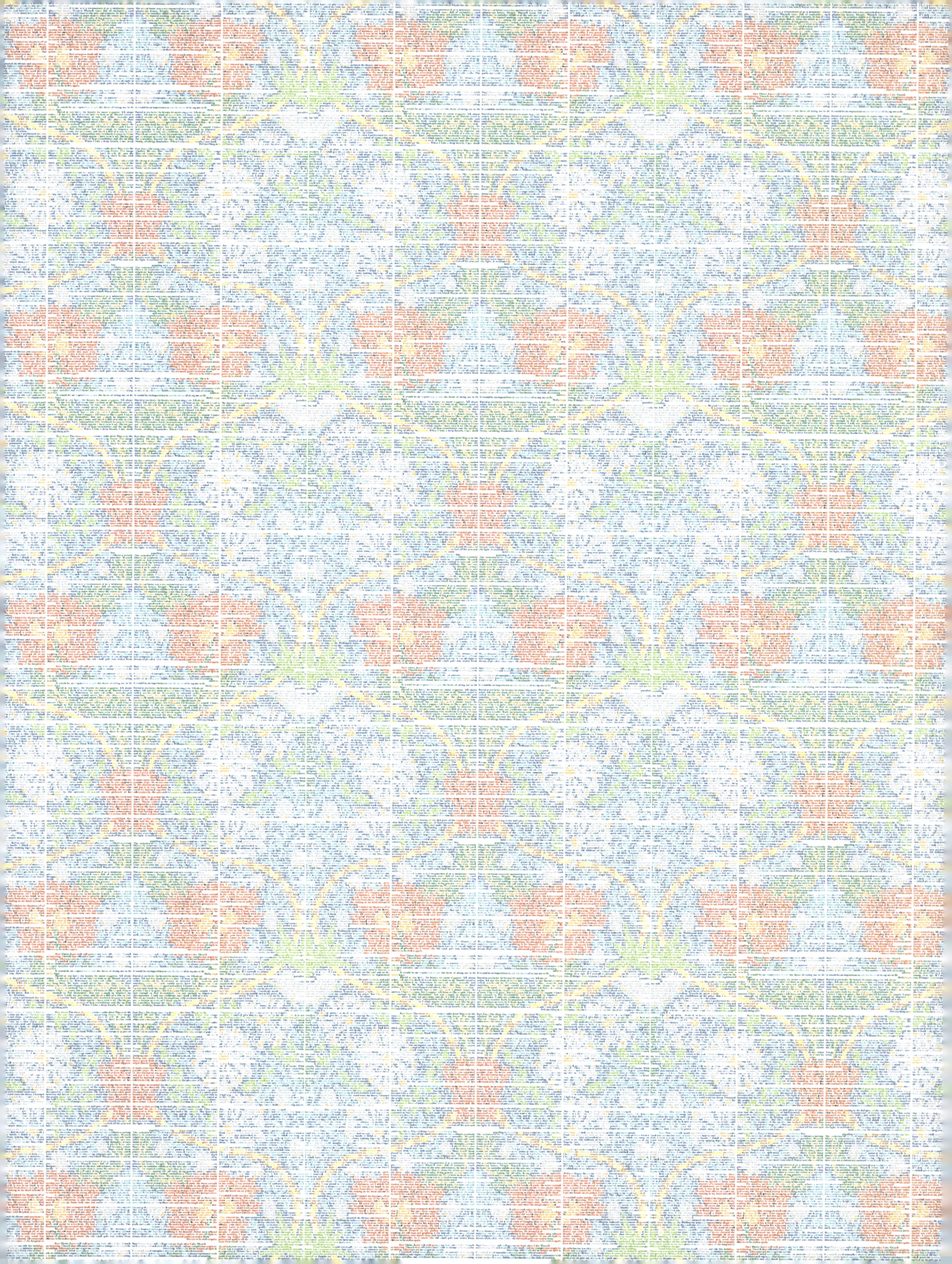

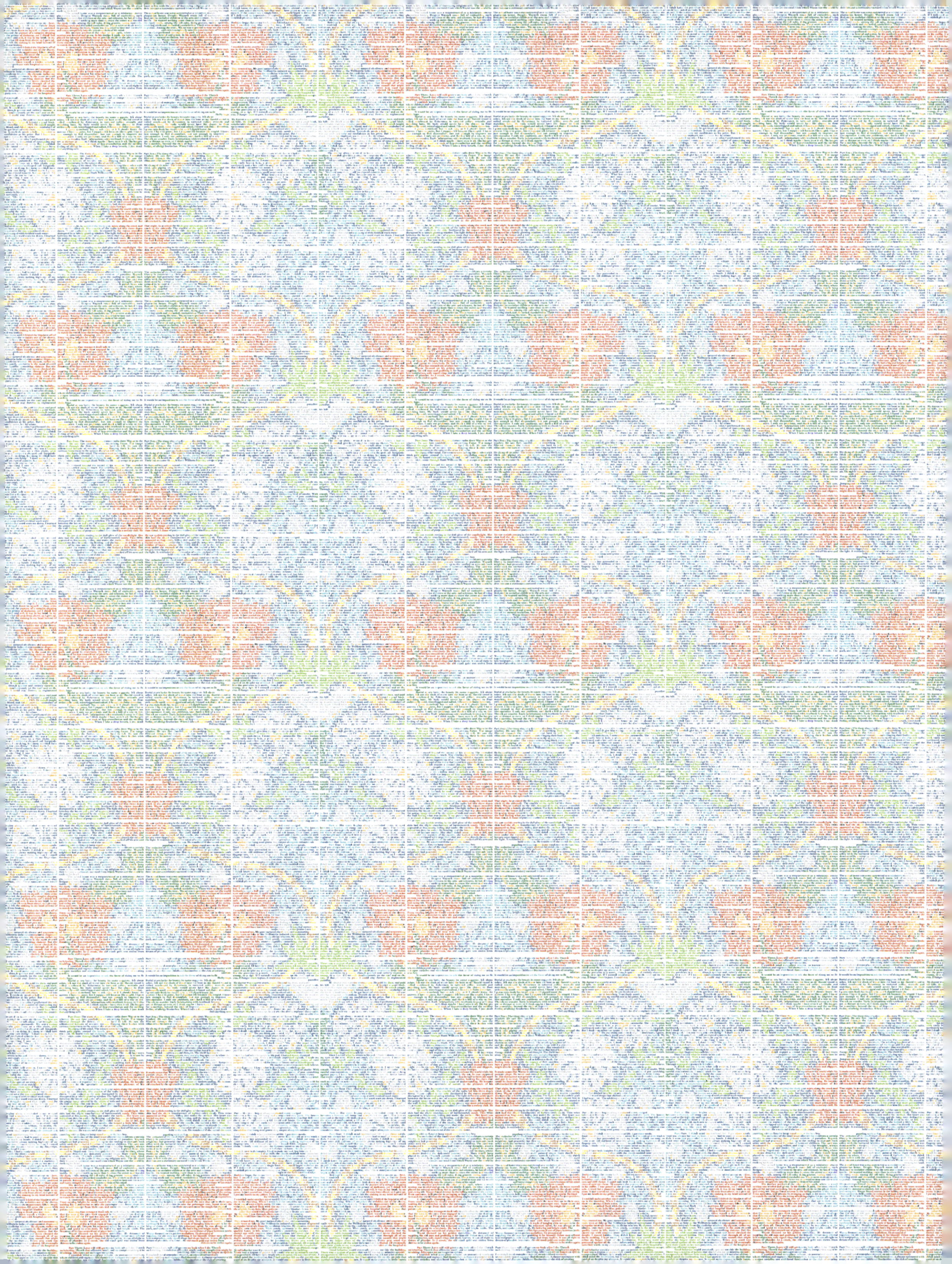

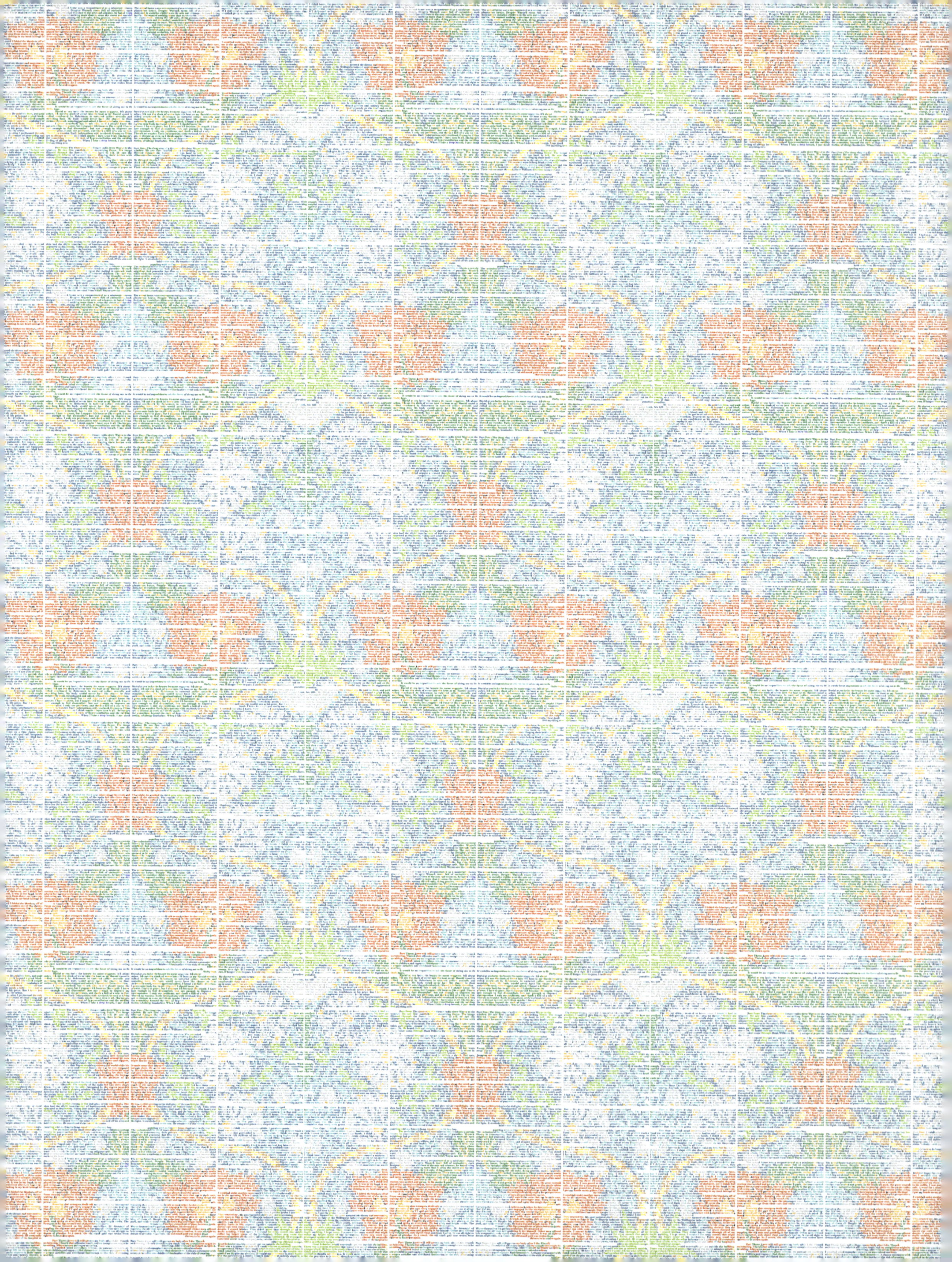

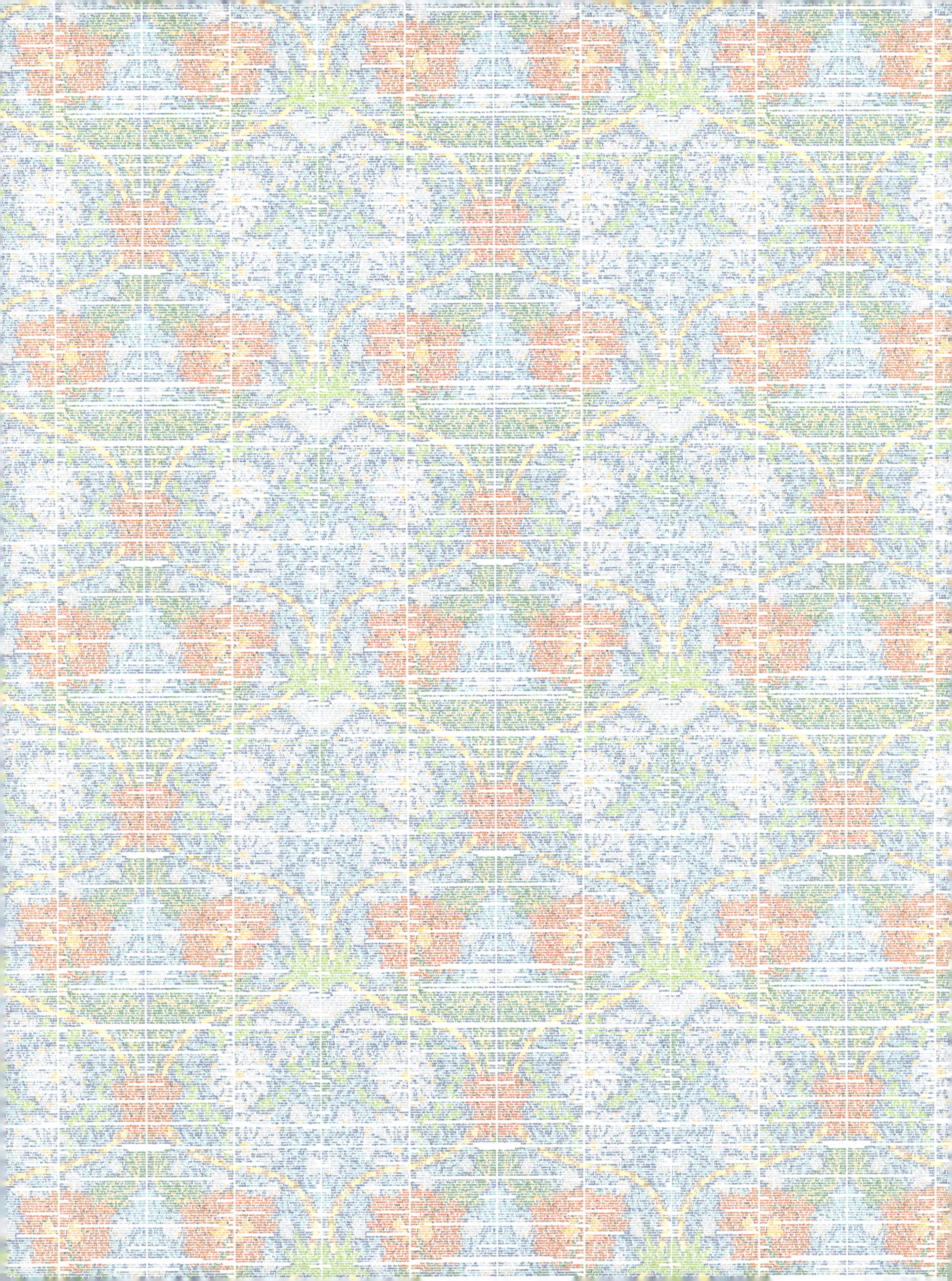

Part One

I didn't mind institutional life. I got three meals. Food was always hot and on time. I never had to cook or even wash a dish. I even just pretended to wash my hands. I didn't use soap, so there were still millions of invisible germs making highways of my fingerprints. I like myself that way. I wasn't filthy, because I seemed clean. Nobody could imagine the diseases latent on my fingertips. Secrets feel close to home, they're all I know.

I didn't have to do laundry. I had to make my bed, but faked it. I didn't let myself toss. I slept still; the sheets couldn't come untucked. I had to suppress my dreams to maintain a faint awareness of my body. I had to override the irrational movements that came out of dreaming. I didn't know the procedure for folding sheets around a mattress. I could have asked anybody, but that would have given up too much of myself. If the nurses saw a single limit, they could begin to define me. If I delivered an impression of maturity and intelligent grace, they wouldn't piece me into something else. Their manipulations would begin at the first unrefined edge.

Bedtime began flat on my back, arms folded across my chest, but I couldn't stay that way for long. I felt the a flutter from levitation, and a dull sense of loss. I couldn't stop it. I tried, panicked eyes and stiff throat. I could only look down on myself, at those arms crossed over my chest. I'd assumed the posture of a vampire sleeping in his coffin. I was posed as the prince of darkness, yet I didn't feel safe. A word for a monster, power and evil, it was in my head, in my room. It just scared me. I knew what I'd seen from above, so I gave up. I put my hands on my pillow. I felt the sinking in my head instead of my stomach. The vampire spell was broken.

I wouldn't make another move until I folded the blankets off of me in the morning. When I stretched the wrinkles out of the sheets, there was always a little extra. I'd leave the unnecessary fabric deeply wrinkled, smashed flush with the mattress. I'd cover the excess with the slightly fuzzy, baby blue, polyester hospital blanket. It was that color that could trick anyone into feeling at home now and then.

By the time I was through, there wasn't a visible wrinkle. Nobody could have known my inexperience with hospital corners. On inspection, I got the praise I needed.

They trusted me. My good natured obedience and unassuming smile were as fake as the Wellbutrin induced contentment dispensed at regular intervals from the medicine window. My shyness, rather my silence, won their trust. With youth, quietness is the most revered quality. Later in life, reserve signifies something sinister. But the nurses ran with common sense assumptions and never checked the details. I stayed hidden. They didn't know that through all of my docile nodding, I kept notes. I scanned for stray sounds that might refine my larger sense of the institution. Every new word was processed against all the other information I gathered. I'd eventually turn their words to my own purposes, use the rules of the hospital to effect an efficient escape.

Good behavior would eventually get me outside the building. There was a system of points that would win me 15 minutes outside, unsupervised. I'd have to be ready when it came; it's not a lot of time. I didn't mind the institution, but I had another life on the outside that carried on despite my absence. It would make contact in little bursts like the previews to a movie, though quicker and entirely visceral, a cramp, or a sigh. If I weren't simultaneously on the trail and on the run, if danger were to pass, I could stay forever in regimented paradise.

My doctor was a pretty average guy. He paid his dues, and paid his bills. He didn't seem like the type to push beyond a good book, comfortable chair and regular contributions to PBS. He wasn't caught up in some quest for a trophy blond, and didn't know the vocabulary of the track. I don't know why he got involved with them. Maybe evil was just his response to boredom. Everybody needs a hobby. He tried to win me over and take my confidence as his prize. But I knew too much. I knew his employer, not by name, but by crime.

I couldn't say what I knew. Every session I performed the role of bored, depressed teenager evading a discussion of consuming and confusing feelings. I was desperate to tell my story. But I couldn't finish. I didn't know how they found me out. It should have been different. Maybe it was a spy in my own head who replaced the cyanide tablets with Pez.

The doctor always wanted to know what I knew. I had to swallow. I couldn't give him enough to assess my threat. "So how are you feeling today?"

"I miss TV."

"Can we talk about what brought you here?"

"An ambulance. I remember the paramedic. She was a woman with curly brown hair, a plain gold cross on a thin chain, pink turtleneck under her uniform and I noticed a chipped nail, burgundy. But I don't remember her name. I was dying, her name wouldn't have done any good."

"Do you think you were dying?"

"I don't know. I guess. No."

"You told somebody you'd swallowed cyanide, but you hadn't. We call that a cry for help. What brought you to that point; what can I help you with?"

"It's just something I saw on TV. Batman or something. The Penguin, I don't know."

"Do you like super-heros?"

"No. I just watch whatever's on, except news. I'll watch anything, it's all the same, something to fill my head, pass the time".

"Eventually, you'll tell me". I filtered through his casually optimistic façade for the intentions that lingered beneath his breath.

Once I asked what he wrote in his pad. I looked down, diverted my eyes to the side. With a nervously aspirated squeak, I made my request. He wasn't convinced. "I'm just keeping notes of your progress". But he received the image of innocence and inadequacy. Through repeated exposure he'd believe.

It didn't matter. I knew what he'd written. I could hear the sounds. They crossed the room like a dissipating trail of smoke. With careful concentration, I could catch the nuances of pen scratching against paper. I knew how to build the sounds into the letter forms that would combine into the doctor's words in my head.

I needed to tell the story, that linoleum. It's grid of squares, each marked by an ochre snowflake against an orange pattern with its sketchy geometric impression of sunburst or sunshine. It was covered by a million tiny, shimmering drops, some sort of liquid Vegas spread thin across the floor. They tried to clean up. They couldn't have known I was coming. Anybody would have assumed it was a freshly cleaned floor. But sloshed into the corner were the tiny coagulated chunks and a few red drops that shifted and merged with residual wash water.

I had to get out. The adolescent ward wore me down. I learned to live inside my head, but I struggled against that stupid need for human interaction. I woke up one morning saying "I love you!" I stood, fully awake, and hugged an armload of air. I pressed it gently with my tongue. My lips closed, holding everything inside.

Part Two

His story begins along a secluded street wedged between a freeway off ramp and a neglected city park. The houses emerged as the typically uniform post war construction that delivered the sense of confinement a GI would call home. Over time, places were bought and sold, each new occupant added to the aesthetic until regiment was lost to traces of eccentric whims. Examining the architecture was like past life regression. The Mediterranean chandelier that hung over green shag carpet alongside colonial oak paneling with an Empire lamp stand next to the lazy boy.

The seclusion of the small tract allowed the residents a certain liberty in constructing their private versions of paradise. Wayne's neighbors had peacocks that flew up to the rooftop to serenade each other with the tortured falsettos of battered children. The yard was dominated by a weeping willow, and despite regular droughts, always seemed to be cool and muddy. The gate to Wayne's picket fence was flanked by Napoleonic lions that guarded the cement bestiary whose residents dwarfed the delicately painted virgin Mary they'd been placed to adore. (Wayne's parents weren't Catholic, but they didn't want to live with the guilt of destroying religious art). The life sized deer became a stationary carousel from which Wayne saw the world by cocking his head.

The actual home was reconstructed as a miniature stucco plantation house. Despite Wayne's room full of curiosities, each designed to socialize children to the arts and sciences, he hated being inside. He wanted nothing more than to cross the street and wander the dusty trails, among the tall oaks, dying grasses, racing squirrels, trickling creek and discarded exoskeletons. There were so many nooks to pursue. Among the trees, Wayne was expected to tune out the world and enter completely into the constructions of his mind.

His mother preferred the edge of the park, where a small section was leveled and green. In his mother's park, the trees weren't placed for natural occlusion, but to provide shade to the picnic tables and swing set. Wayne found retreat in the lulling motion of the swing. Even nauseous, he'd persist in swinging as high as he could. He liked to watch the world, mistaking angles for perspectives.

A constantly changing row of cars always lined the street. From varying heights he would watch the men that sat in their cars, waiting for a pedestrian to take the passenger seat. Some times the men would emerge from their cars and enter the rough shrubs and poison oak.

Knowing that strangers don't talk to each other, he determined that the men in the cars were engaged in the surreptitious dealings that filtered off the TV and out into the world through his mind. He heard their discussions of stolen gold, counterfeit bills and other sorts of booty. The feeble old man with liver spotted hands, whose turtleneck looked like a fresh wash of hanging skin seemed to be the king of them all. Despite his reluctant spine, he was always at the park, and spoke to everybody. He had a big and bright smile. The firmness of his lips seemed out of place between jowls.

Wayne focused on the golden medallion. He dreamed of toppling the old man and grabbing it for himself. Other men offered less temptation, only signet rings and dusty loafers. It was all right to dream of plunder. As a crook, the old man's gold was stolen from thieves to be stolen again.

Part Three

Laws will still govern my body after I die. There's no loitering. There's that offensive smell, and my complexion might be troubling. Alleyways are no longer an option.

I wouldn't mind someplace remote, an unresolved territory where children and vagrants find themselves. A chance encounter with a corpse satisfies one childhood fascination at the risk of creating another.

It would be an imposition to ask the favor of sizing me to fit Hefty bags.

Burial at sea lacks the beauty its name suggests. It's about ashes. It's not the slosh of water into the boat as my flaccid vessel is rolled overboard by fishermen in tattered yellow overalls and matching hats. My body would never have the chance to float awkwardly until, waterlogged and salted, I found a definite direction.

I guess somebody has to ask why, as if I should know the answer. I have to guess, but I suppose it's because I'm stupid. I know just enough to feel discomfort, but not enough to improve my circumstance. I only see problems, and that's a hell of a way to live. There's no wonder. Early infatuations with textbook Greece or China are as distant as ever, so I think maybe I have seen it all. I'm hungry for something beyond the rush of hyperventilation and the sublime feeling of allergy headaches. When I take a deep breath, I just don't feel anything new.

Part Four

The tinny ring of a distant radio drew Wayne to the window. He saw fire: candlelight or something fierce. The image filtered through the forest, so it was hard to tell. He saw the silhouetted breasts of ecstatic women flinging their bodies with cartoon limberness to the satanic din of an AM radio.

He changed his mind. The women were in long black robes with thick gold piping around the hoods, pacing crestfallen around the stone pit. He heard their call dodging in and out of Cool Clear Waters. Their voices came through Hank Williams like tiny scraps of paper on the floor.

He focused beyond the sound of his window. The corroded aluminum rattled along its track. The whirling laughter of the cicadas and the deeply drawn comments of the frogs added a viscosity to the air. Though it was an impression of a voice that traveled like a secret code within the sound of the radio that lured him onto the lawn.

Escape didn't require a second thought. The thrill had worn away. The world of mosquitoes, rats and playing opossum is where he felt safe. Wayne found a strange comfort in red eyes and buzzing.

Jumping out his window used to deliver a shock. But now, feeling only came with the impact of feet smashing dark footprints into a green field of tiny pearls. The suction of mud around his toes might also be enough. Thoughts of warmth, bed sheets and slippers, flashed so rapidly through his head, they became foreign.

It made sense that Wayne would experience the world while his parents slept. He never understood family the way he was supposed to. His discontent was greatest at night, when he had to focus his mind and put it to rest. Instead, he would wander, looking for clues that could be fastened together for a sense of understanding. He became sidetracked by the spectacle of nature in the pleasure of his abandonment.

That night, he avoided the thick gray mists along the creek and stuck to the sidewalk. The crackle of the radio led him three doors down. Wayne walked to the side, fascinated by the stucco monolith disrupted by a faintly glowing window. The light defined a subtle path between the house and a row of cypress trees that was almost lost in the grainy image created by the strain of rods and cones. He stared at the wall feeling what was inside. X-ray power was more premonitory than visual. A sense of purpose washed over him like a sweaty chill. He felt at ease.

He saw eyelids resting in the dull glow of the candlelight. Her skin had the slight translucency of butterscotch candy. Thin veins appeared as fragments, hiding just under the surface. Her heart was buried too deep to notice the beating, and the lungs were defined by a residue of incense smoke. Her chest didn't seem to rise or fall, and even under the warmth of the candle, she looked a little blue. Her breasts were tipped with large blots that seemed to absorb the color of the light. It reminded him of the color of scabs, sucked off his arm and held to the sun. He wondered if she tasted the same.

Bird & Anenome
after William Morris

Part One: I sit at the edge of her bed feeling numb but sore, desperate for those answers that leave questions in their wake. That's what love is about, wanting to know who she is, what's there when everything else is gone, when her eyes are black and vacant staring up toward some forgotten thought that might make things alright. I want the kind of answers that can only be found while she sleeps, a twitching foot or a quick snort of air. I collect her details and insinuate myself into her past. I'm making her story; she's nothing outside my conclusion. But that does make me to blame. I'm responsible for the scar that's now nearly invisible along the side of her chin. A fall down the stairs, an accident at swim practice, unfortunate fallout from a younger brother's practical joke, I put it there to remind me of what I want.

I've never seen her eyes flutter off to sleep. They're closed when I arrive. I crawl so softly on to her bed, she never knows when I've come. If she feels me at all, I'm a veil over her dream. I'm just the movement of a cloud.

I stare too hard at the diffused patterns reflected from her forehead and the deep pores in her nose. The gestalt of flesh and blood falters. Dissolution is a feeling, and she's just a background. Everything important is engulfed in static. Her face is drawn in dark felt against the off-black space of the world. There's nothing mundane left for her to shine against. So maybe I have seen heaven.

There can't be an exchange. I'm too much an alchemist, scratching out the world and inscribing my sense in its place. It all dissolves into the mental equivalent of a chemical burn. The layers don't make sense. The pieces are all there, but I can't force them into something beautiful. Memory becomes a series of viscous trails, glossy and gory. Nothing comes to the point.

I'm so familiar with her plumbing. I know the tiniest leaks, the soft texture of solder, the bad repair that will give again, that stuttering early morning tap. I've mapped the bends and splits of her pipes and cataloged the sound of it all draining away.

I wait behind the wall. I live along that expressway between kitchen and bath. I wonder if she ever listens to the blank haze of the world intently enough to hear my nose scrape the backside of her baseboard, and the slight ring when my hand releases a pipe.

I know where to look for gagging and heaving. She leaves the medicine cabinet open, so I watch her through an unused screw hole. I see her doubled on the floor and wonder why I don't even want to help. But that's not how it is. I can only pull her into me. Her destruction doesn't matter, that's what I make of her anyway. She uses the toilet to pull herself up, sways about the room and checks her hair before staggering back to her bedroom. That's when I get mine.

Her clean up is more like painting. She leaves me what I need, on the floor, in the random bits that had a short life inside her. I can taste the difference between alcoholism and bulimia.

I don't have so much to work with, so my mouth is important. My hands are too callused to appreciate the soft possibilities of shoulders and legs. My sense of smell is heightened so her various floral scents disgust me.

She hit me. The memory emerges slowly from someplace I don't recognize. The sun started to rise and the red orange melancholic glow stained the room. My mouth was close to her toe. Maybe I wanted to feel the shallow ridges in her skin bump against my teeth. Maybe my tongue pushed out for a sense of what she inadvertently collects. I knew she would be up soon and off to work. I'm always left behind. I thought so hard, "Just stay" and I don't know how, but it came out "Justine" and it resounded like thunder echoing off of craggy cliffs fading into some cold abyss and startling her from sleep. She kicked me. I remember the strain on my back that I felt in my stomach, and the sting as blood rushed to my face. I looked up from the floor with a childlike wonder. The salty metallic taste was hers, not mine.

Her bare foot rushed toward my face. I watched it like a slow motion trail of yellow that had the distinct presence of summer roses and the smell of cut grass. I knew it was over, but instead of scampering off through my hole in her wall, I stared up defiantly. "I've been in your most private places, seen what you hide at the bottom of that drawer. I've gnawed through silks and lycra, nylon and devoured stained cottons. I know things you don't even know about yourself. I've tasted the softest pinks you have."

Part Two: How did midnight become so dreary? It used to be a rite of passage, a symbol of endurance, a sign of growing up, that feeling that tricks kids into believing they can make their way in the world, that everything will be fine. But I've been up four nights, I think. And I just don't know where to go from here. I want to keep going, to feel the infinite, some sense of pure speed. Freefall. I want to feel like my own momentum is forever. But there isn't a jump high enough, or a chemist alive who can deliver that kind of intensity. I'm alone in a crappy studio apartment on one of the wrong sides of Hollywood. The air is too thick with smoke. The plumes that should be swirling off my cigarette don't show any shape at all; the new trails blend seamlessly with what's already in the air. I guess it just makes me glad I never check the batteries in the smoke detector. Despite all the particles floating around the room, staining the walls, invading the sheets with their gross, comforting smell, there isn't enough of anything to return the high that propelled me through the last few days.

I think I was thinking about love, how men come in small increments, four or five times a day, but still, they're completely elusive. Maybe I just ended up there because I lost track of what I was thinking. I do that. Time gets confused, so when I first heard the soft knocks at my door, I was thrown into a series of questions that had to play out in my head before I could open up. I thought that the knocks, being simply vibration, may have come from another apartment, drifted through space, and become amplified by vibrating the smoke particles that fill my room. Maybe it's the sound, the vibration that's breaking down the stuff that gets me high, and if only the whole world could just shut up for a few minutes, I'll be back on track.

I tried to think who might be knocking at each door in the apartment, but I'm the only one with frequent midnight visitors. So maybe I was wrong, and instead of amplifying, the smoke is like a blanket, muffling a heavy pounding at my own door.

Then there's the typical paranoia that I had to process before I could make a move. I think I paid rent, or my mom paid it or it's been paid somehow. It wouldn't be the landlord coming to take the door in for repairs, leaving me vulnerable to whatever's out there, vulnerable to whatever might come knocking. That's what my landlord wants, to leave me exposed so that one day on his way back from getting the paper, the old man across the hall will look into my space and see me masturbating on a pile of blankets, listening to Madonna, probably. The landlord's goal is to make me so embarrassed that I wouldn't dare show my face in the building, ever again. I don't have any stuff left, so if it's the police, I'm OK. They can't arrest me for the smoke, I don't think. It's mostly from cigarettes anyway. I mean it's not even enough to keep me high. Besides, I wouldn't mind sucking off a cop or two, especially if they're hung. Besides, they would have broken down the door by now, I guess, Like on Law and Order, "Damn it Lenny, We're too late"

Maybe I have done something. Fuck, what have I done? I haven't seen the man across the hall, the one with the glassy eye. It's been a week. Maybe I haven't been outside in four days, of was it five. That's only two days unaccounted for, and maybe that was a weekend, if that matters.

I think I'm safe. If I did something, I'm sure I covered it up in such a clever and exacting way, no detail would be unattended. The cover up would be so perfect that no loose end could spur me to remember my own crime.

I think I might have floated across the bedroom floor. I seem to remember an image of The Visitation from childhood, where you can tell the angel is floating, because its feet are pointing down. I don't know why I'm remembering shit from a docent tour of a crappy museum in third grade. But my toes were curled, and my calves tightened and when I landed across the room, I was surprised to see that I wasn't the angel, but had jeans on instead.

I opened the door, and it was just dark, nothing else.

So I put in a porno and sat back on my bed. I don't even remember the trick to day ratio, but I'll definitely been a horny boy. I don't know if I was horny so much, or I just knew that I couldn't get hard, and it just made me want to fuck like a dirty dog, because I knew I couldn't. It made me wish I could afford both speed and Viagra, but then I thought about this porn star that I started calling Lance Pounder. I don't know his real name, or even his porn name. (I skip the credits because they make me cum before the movie starts, and it sucks to be bored watching porn.) I just like watching the way Lance takes charge, pushing guys here and there until they're exposed and vulnerable. I wouldn't even care if he were looking out for my safety, as long as he owned me. As long as all the responsibility for me being who I am comes back to rest in his arms.

In perfect synchronization with Lance, there was a pounding at the window. I thought it was weird, like a sitcom rendition of Romeo and Juliet or something. It did remind me to check the TV listings, to see what's on later, because now and then, I do need a break from Lance Pounding. There's nothing on except the Golden Girls, and that short sassy one gives me the creeps. Just like that old man. Maybe he was lost in a senile daze and came knocking at my window. If I opened the blinds with a compulsive slowness, the light of the room would spill out onto his crazy eye. And the light would know where to go. It wouldn't light anything else, not a potted flower or a single blade of grass. It would just be drawn to his eye. Those things, things of horror, they're after my space, they want to invade me, and wear me like a suit. They are things of horror trying to take me down from the inside, but I won't let that happen.

So I filter back through all my thoughts of cops and landlords, and the amplifying powers of smoke. Once I see myself as the angel, I know it's OK to open the window. And I do, but then I think I bounced through too many thoughts of bathrobes and bed sheets or I was stuck in a Greek paradox where my mind was only moving, but the things around me did too or something. Fuck! I forget. I don't know why, but I just need to explain to myself why I heard the knocking so distinctly, yet there was only darkness, the same cracked sidewalk, a porch light and the pea green color of the apartment, and nothing more.

So I stood still like a predator, waiting for the thing that haunted me. I flattened myself up against the wall, next to the window, and waited to pounce. My skin faded to match the white of the wall, and my own features became indistinct bits of texture. I monitored my breathing to keep it slow enough to avoid detection. I counted my breaths while timing their duration. And then came the only sound in the world that hadn't become a part of me, and I jumped, ripping down the shade and there he is, an angelic face in a baseball cap, or perhaps my downfall.

I open the window, and he asks if I'm still looking to hook up. I do a lot of cruising on the phone lines, and the internet, but I don't remember inviting anybody over, so I'm suspicious. He could be anybody. I have to keep an eye on him. He may know my darkest secrets or my landlord. He's an agent of the man with the crazy eye! Damn! Why am I remembering so much with a spy in the room trying to make his way into my head. I'll play it so cool, he'll think I'm just any old phone trick. I'll show him.

"Come around to the door and I'll suck your dick."

I walked him to the bed, and remembered that the cat pissed there a few days ago, but it's got to be dry by now. I let her outside after that. Shit! He probably can't smell it anyway with all the smoke in the room. He pulls his pants down just far enough for business, and I play along. By the time I look up the porno is over. I lost track of time, I guess. I do get into sucking cock, and spy or not, he has a nice one. I started to get nervous, because he hadn't come. He didn't reach down to jerk himself or anything. He was enjoying it. He was just watching, trying to decode my performance to see the anxiety I kept so well hidden. He knows that the longer it takes, the weaker I'll get. And then I heard the knocking. It wasn't the door or the window, the landlord or this guy's beating heart. It was coming from the floorboards, and he just sat there with his hands behind his head, eyes closed, and a smug smile. I could hear the old man's beating heart and that sound, coupled with my horror soothed this sick fucker.

So I bit him. I know he is bleeding because I can taste it. But before he can scream, I am already at the closet, grabbing a crowbar. "Tear up the floor boards; you'll find the old man there."

Part Three: I can feel the tumor in my chest. I know its position. It presses my ribs near the sternum and I can feel its depth. I know how far it presses into my lungs, and how hard it pushes against the bones. It's a perfect image of its shape as it spreads between organs. I can imagine the black pustule, feeding from my veins. My beating heart feeds the disease. It's insides are just as soft and silky pink as my own. It just has more yellow-green, that hue that never signifies beauty.

A doctor might tell me I've got a year to live. No more than a year. But that seems like enough. I know time escapes me, but I'm not doing so much. I've never found my thing. I looked for meaning in the usual places: art, love, poetry, medicine, invention, religion. They all came up empty. Just empty. And so I wonder what I am if the external world fails. How can I be about nothing, because if I'm not defined, what am I? So yes, a year in this body seems like plenty.

I understand the body's propensity to self regulate. I've learned how to interpret the systems that keep my body running. I know the warning signs. They come up like red lights on the dashboard. I can't deny a single craving, because my body tells me what I need. I can quantify disease to determine how long a fever will last. I just have to pause myself until I am so still I can hear in my heart the harsh revving of a machine. I can feel the flow of blood in the tiniest capillaries. I analyze my body's chemistry, determine deficiencies and restore the balance.

I'm scared in a way that doesn't allow me to plan for the future. I don't know how to spend the days. What can I make myself into? What kind of person do I want to be when I die? It feels like pop rocks under my skin, or maybe the bubbles in soda that shoot above the rim of the glass. Maybe they've just joined into a fatal combination. The feeling is a distinct fizzle. Nothing hits a nerve, so I don't cry out. There's no pain, just the tingling knowledge of a disease. It's just the feeling of tiny fibers in my muscles giving way, being pushed aside by a malignant growth. It's just below the skin, I can feel it pressing up against the roots of hairs, and pushing down through the muscles.

We understand life by the potential for death, but it's another thing to feel it happening. Mortality is no longer an abstract; it's shifted from its place in the shadows. It's no longer darkness, but a distant illumination. But still there's nothing waiting for me. The light on the other side is just an empty promise of warmth.

I spent a half hour grieving. I didn't have to look at the clock. On my back, tears tickled my cheeks, then my ears. I tried to understand the effect of my death among family and friends. My mother's sense of the world was bound up in my smile. I guess her dreams will be gone, though it's more to do with her than me. I can see my father's smug expression. He doesn't yet know how haunting victory can be. My sister doesn't understand. She doesn't understand change. It's just that my number will be disconnected and there will be no replacement. I think she's afraid of pragmatism. Smaller changes have sent her into violent rages. I feel sorry for her dog.

It all made sense in a heady rush. I understood the tumor. I remembered how often he cooked for me, the dark bottle on the counter. He said it was gin, but there wasn't a label. Then that damn missing water bill. And the messes he leaves in the living room. He thinks he can drive me crazy. He's poisoning me and he thinks, I won't even notice the toxins taking me down. He thinks I'll just succumb, without a word, without a thought. And he's sleeping so soundly next to me, the pleasure in his face as he enjoys a fucking dream.

He's using something like arsenic, something that builds up over time, but it can't be so conventional. He's not a risk taker. And he's smarter than that. He must have involved a chemist. It has to be something new, specific and undetectable. I'm not even going to make it through the night. I'll never get to tell my story. Nobody will ever know. I'll just be another sheet of concrete in a procession of monuments built to allow forgetting. I just don't know where to start. I've become too weak to crawl to the bathroom, yet I have this reserve of anger. So I'll rest, still like a spider, waiting for the springs to move. When I feel his gentle pulsing through the mattress, I'll pounce. I'll grab him by the throat. My two thumbs should have just enough pressure to take him with me.

Part Four: The scenes of Goya are gouged and smeared at the bottom of the door. It's all smoke and limbs. Nature isn't even left standing. Just the door.

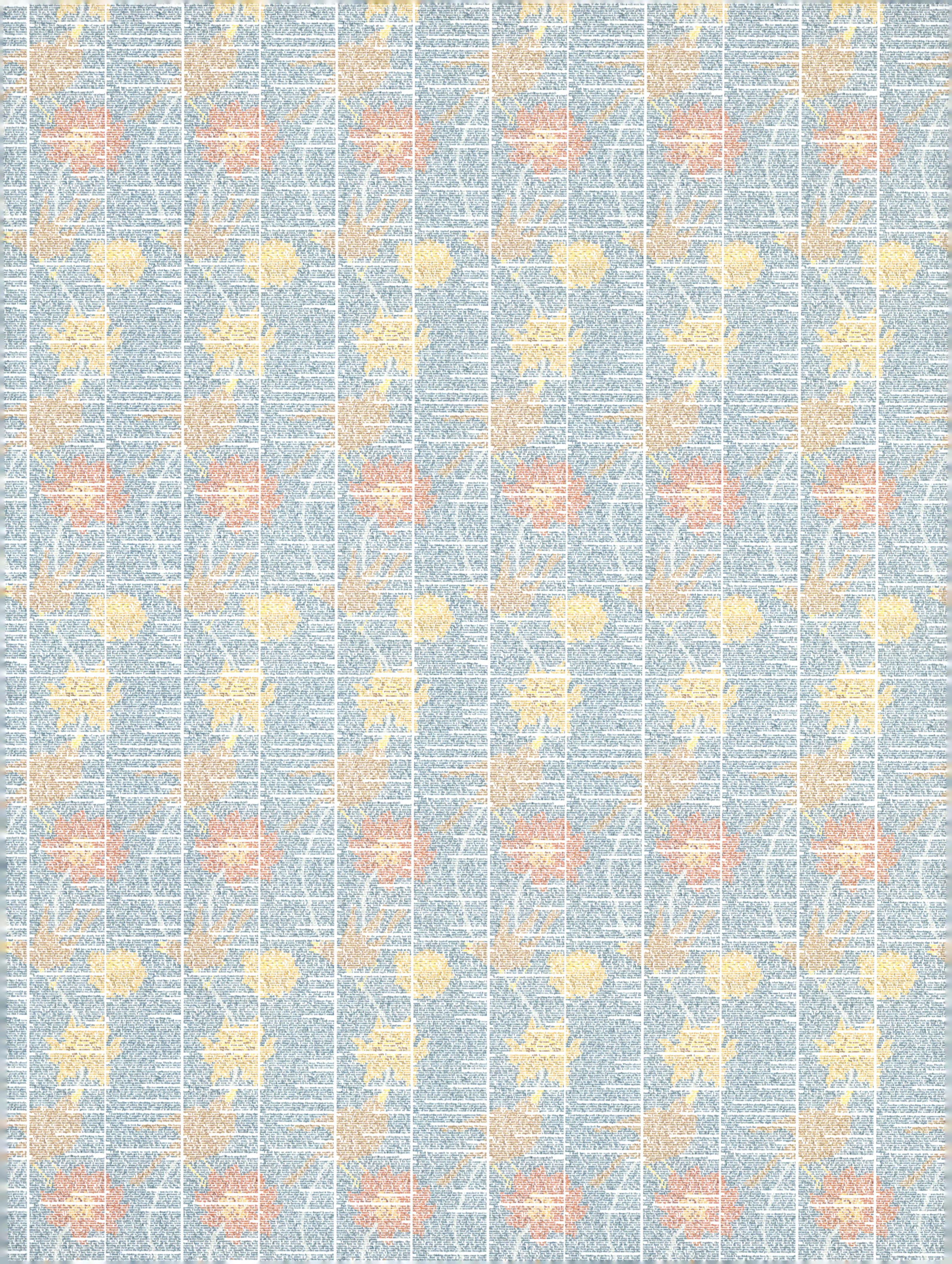

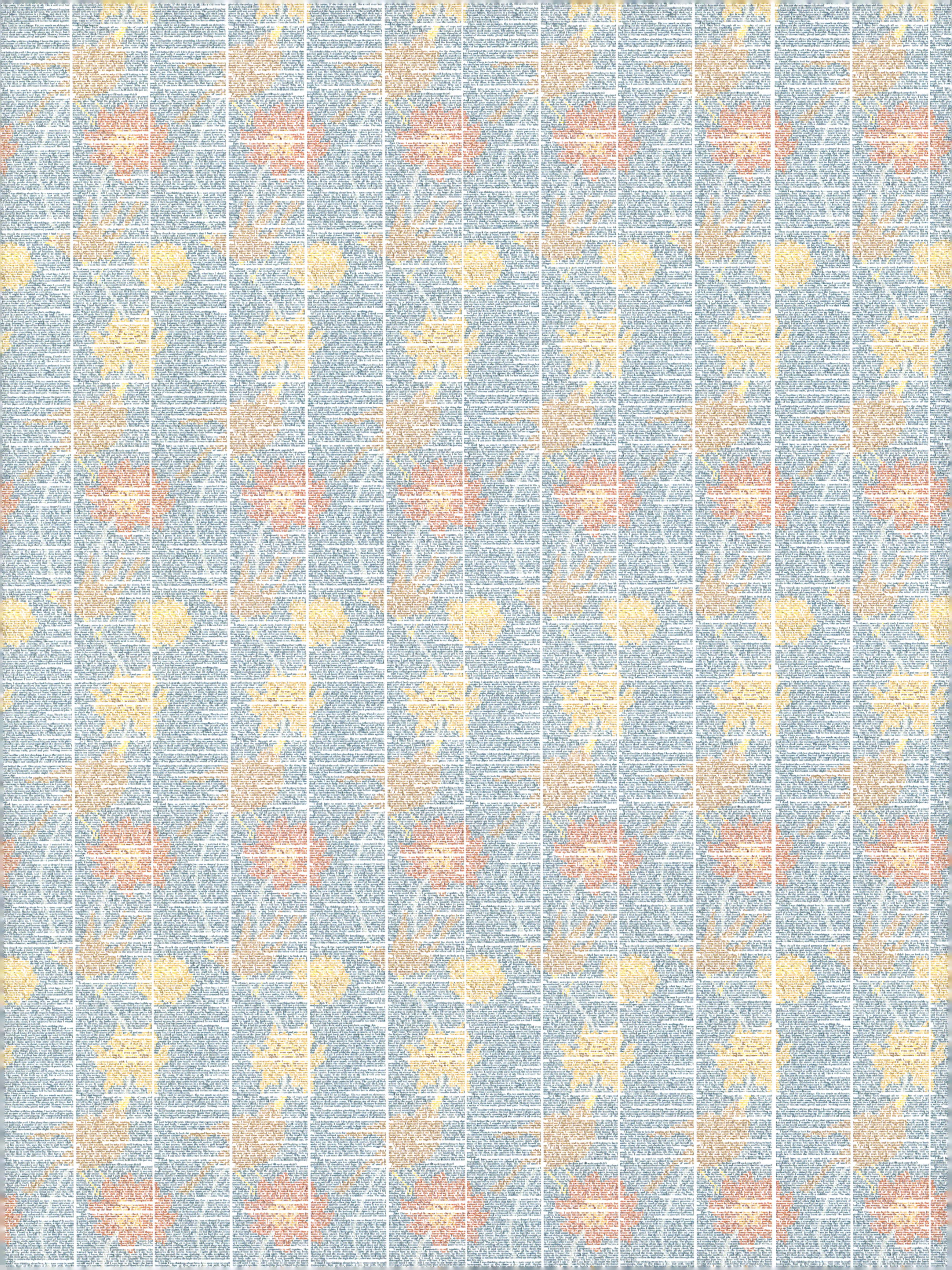

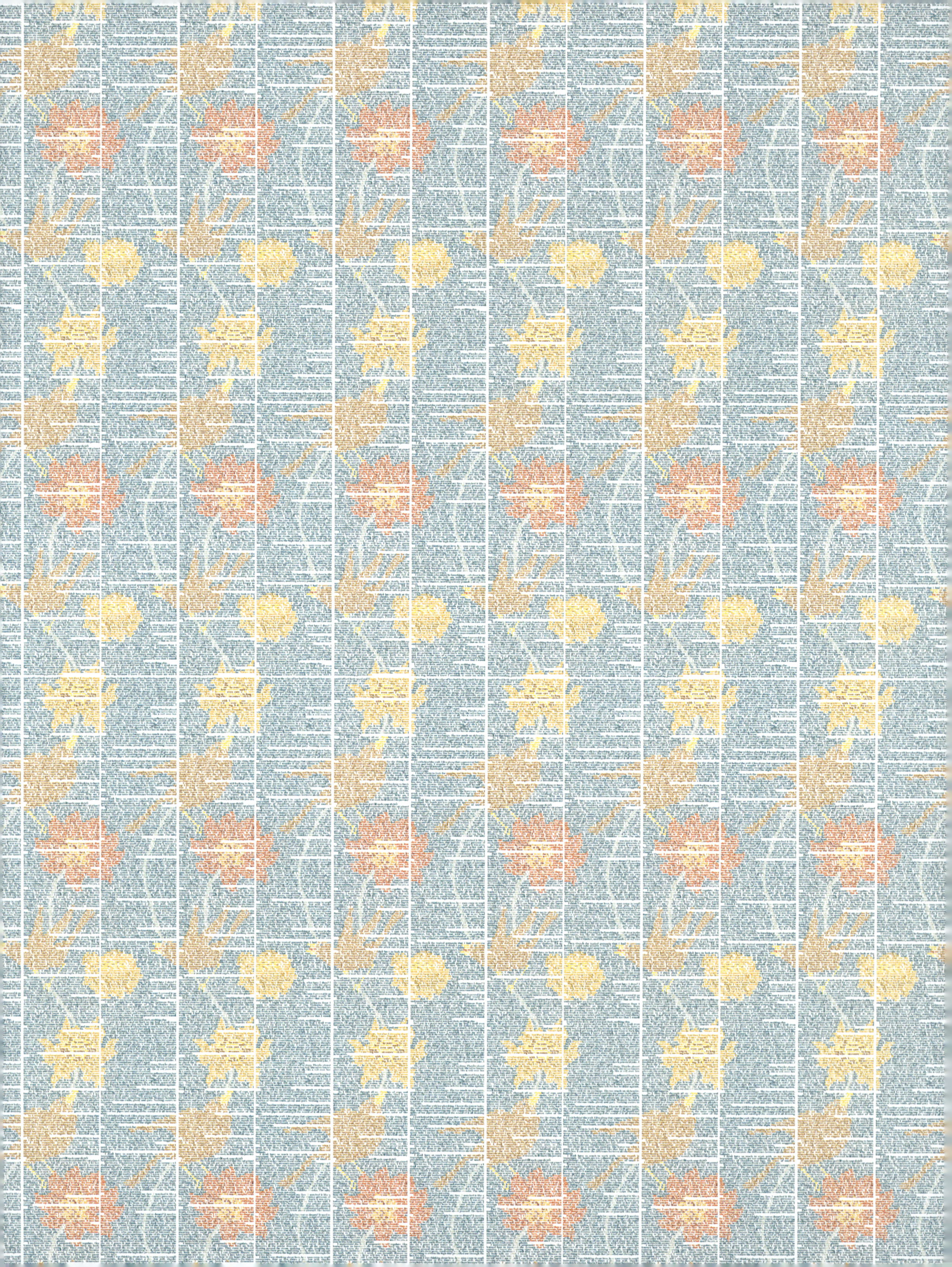

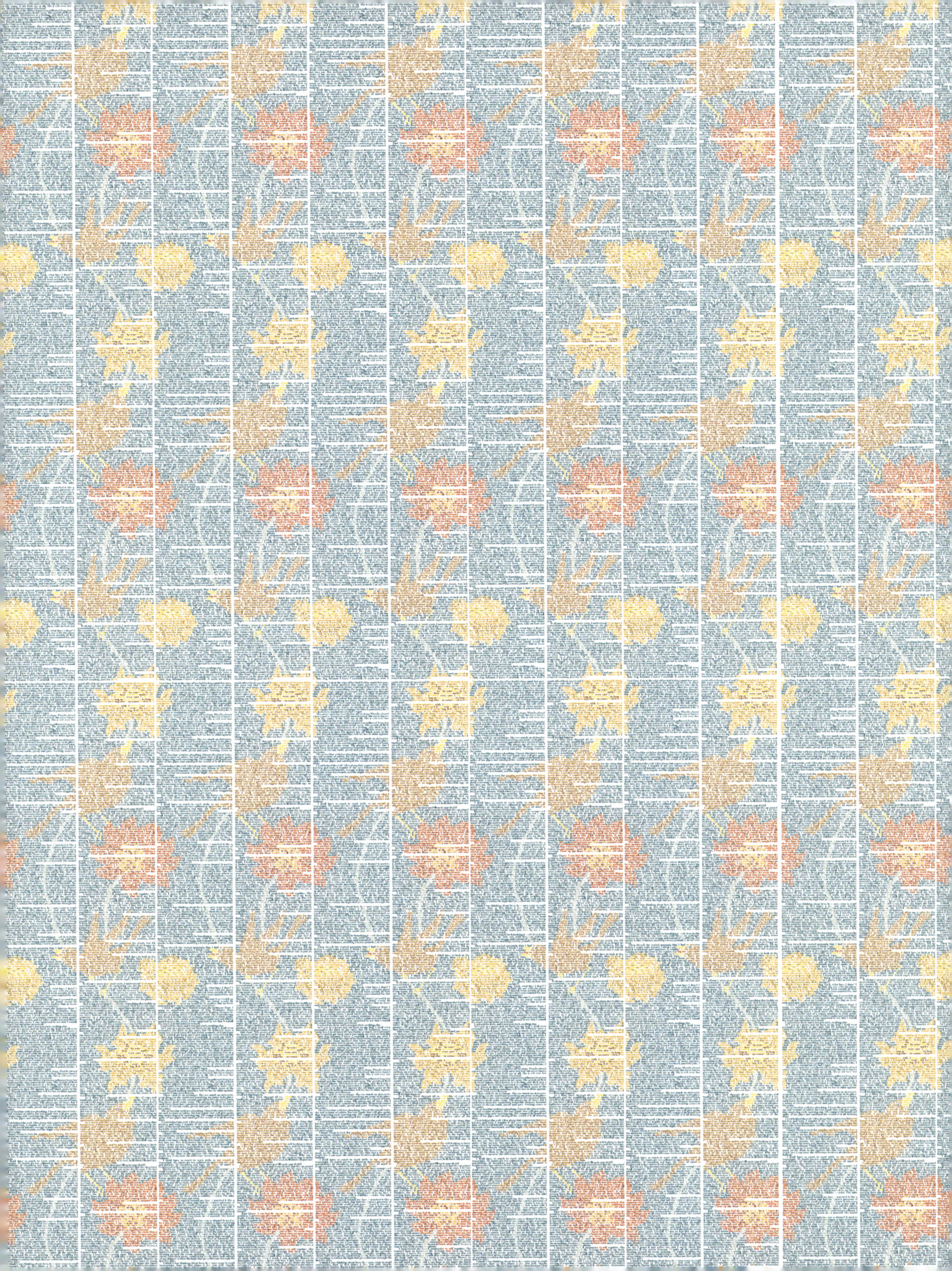

Part One

I sit at the edge of her bed feeling numb but sore, desperate for those answers that leave questions in their wake. That's what love is about, wanting to know who she is, what's there when everything else is gone, when her eyes are black and vacant staring up toward some forgotten thought that might make things alright. I want the kind of answers that can only be found while she sleeps, a twitching foot or a quick snort of air. I collect her details and insinuate myself into her past. I'm making her story; she's nothing outside my conclusion. But that does make me to blame. I'm responsible for the scar that's now nearly invisible along the side of her chin. A fall down the stairs, an accident at swim practice, unfortunate fallout from a younger brother's practical joke, I put it there to remind me of what I want.

I've never seen her eyes flutter off to sleep. They're closed when I arrive. I crawl so softly on to her bed, she never knows when I've come. If she feels me at all, I'm a veil over her dream. I'm just the movement of a cloud.

I stare too hard at the diffused patterns reflected from her forehead and the deep pores in her nose. The gestalt of flesh and blood falters. Dissolution is a feeling, and she's just a background. Everything important is engulfed in static. Her face is drawn in dark felt against the off-black space of the world. There's nothing mundane left for her to shine against. So maybe I have seen heaven.

There can't be an exchange. I'm too much an alchemist, scratching out the world and inscribing my sense in its place. It all dissolves into the mental equivalent of a chemical burn. The layers don't make sense. The pieces are all there, but I can't force them into something beautiful. Memory becomes a series of viscous trails, glossy and gory. Nothing comes to the point.

I'm so familiar with her plumbing. I know the tiniest leaks, the soft texture of solder, the bad repair that will give again, that stuttering early morning tap. I've mapped the bends and splits of her pipes and cataloged the sound of it all draining away.

I wait behind the wall. I live along that expressway between kitchen and bath. I wonder if she ever listens to the blank haze of the world intently enough to hear my nose scrape the backside of her baseboard, and the slight ring when my hand releases a pipe.

I know where to look for gagging and heaving. She leaves the medicine cabinet open, so I watch her through an unused screw hole. I see her doubled on the floor and wonder why I don't even want to help. But that's not how it is. I can only pull her into me. Her destruction doesn't matter, that's what I make of her anyway. She uses the toilet to pull herself up, sways about the room and checks her hair before staggering back to her bedroom. That's when I get mine.

Her clean up is more like painting. She leaves me what I need, on the floor, in the random bits that had a short life inside her. I can taste the difference between alcoholism and bulimia.

I don't have so much to work with, so my mouth is important. My hands are too callused to appreciate the soft possibilities of shoulders and legs. My sense of smell is heightened so her various floral scents disgust me.

She hit me. The memory emerges slowly from someplace I don't recognize. The sun started to rise and the red orange melancholic glow stained the room. My mouth was close to her toe. Maybe I wanted to feel the shallow ridges in her skin bump against my teeth. Maybe my tongue pushed out for a sense of what she inadvertently collects. I knew she would be up soon and off to work. I'm always left behind. I thought so hard, "Just stay" and I don't know how, but it came out "Justine" and it resounded like thunder echoing off of craggy cliffs fading into some cold abyss and startling her from sleep.

She kicked me. I remember the strain on my back that I felt in my stomach, and the sting as blood rushed to my face. I looked up from the floor with a childlike wonder. The salty metallic taste was hers, not mine.

Her bare foot rushed toward my face. I watched it like a slow motion trail of yellow that had the distinct presence of summer roses and the smell of cut grass. I knew it was over, but instead of scampering off through my hole in her wall, I stared up defiantly. "I've been in your most private places, seen what you hide at the bottom of that drawer. I've gnawed through silks and lycra, nylon and devoured stained cottons. I know things you don't even know about yourself. I've tasted the softest pinks you have."

Part Two

How did midnight become so dreary? It used to be a rite of passage, a symbol of endurance, a sign of growing up, that feeling that tricks kids into believing they can make their way in the world, that everything will be fine. But I've been up four nights, I think. And I just don't know where to go from here. I want to keep going, to feel the infinite, some sense of pure speed. Freefall. I want to feel like my own momentum is forever. But there isn't a jump high enough, or a chemist alive who can deliver that kind of intensity. I'm alone in a crappy studio apartment on one of the wrong sides of Hollywood. The air is too thick with smoke. The plumes that should be swirling off my cigarette don't show any shape at all; the new trails blend seamlessly with what's already in the air. I guess it just makes me glad I never check the batteries in the smoke detector. Despite all the particles floating around the room, staining the walls, invading the sheets with their gross, comforting smell, there isn't enough of anything to return the high that propelled me through the last few days.

I think I was thinking about love, how men come in small increments, four or five times a day, but still, they're completely elusive. Maybe I just ended up there because I lost track of what I was thinking. I do that. Time gets confused, so when I first heard the soft knocks at my door, I was thrown into a series of questions that had to play out in my head before I could open up. I thought that the knocks, being simply vibration, may have come from another apartment, drifted through space, and become amplified by vibrating the smoke particles that fill my room. Maybe it's the sound, the vibration that's breaking down the stuff that gets me high, and if only the whole world could just shut up for a few minutes, I'd be back on track.

I tried to think who might be knocking at each door in the apartment, but I'm the only one with frequent midnight visitors. So maybe I was wrong, and instead of amplifying, the smoke is like a blanket, muffling a heavy pounding at my own door.

Then there's the typical paranoia that I had to process before I could make a move. I think I paid rent, or my mom paid it or it's been paid somehow. It wouldn't be the landlord coming to take the door in for repairs, leaving me vulnerable to whatever's out there, vulnerable to whatever might come knocking. That's what my landlord wants, to leave me exposed so that one day on his way back from getting the paper, the old man across the hall will look into my space and see me masturbating on a pile of blankets, listening to Madonna, probably. The landlord's goal is to make me so embarrassed that I wouldn't dare show my face in the building, ever again. I don't have any stuff left, so if it's the police, I'm OK. They can't arrest me for the smoke, I don't think. It's mostly from cigarettes anyway. I mean it's not even enough to keep me high. Besides, I wouldn't mind sucking off a cop or two, especially if they're hung. Besides, they would have broken down the door by now, I guess, like on Law and Order, "Damn it Lenny, We're too late".

Maybe I have done something. Fuck, what have I done? I haven't seen the man across the hall, the one with the glassy eye. It's been a week. Maybe I haven't been outside in four days, of was it five. That's only two days unaccounted for, and maybe that was a weekend, if that matters.

I think I'm safe. If I did something, I'm sure I covered it up in such a clever and exacting way, no detail would be unattended. The cover up would be so perfect that no loose end could spur me to remember my own crime.

I think I might have floated across the bedroom floor. I seem to remember an image of The Visitation from childhood, where you can tell the angel is floating, because its feet are pointing down. I don't know why I'm remembering shit from a docent tour of a crappy museum in third grade. But my toes were curled, and my calves tightened and when I landed across the room, I was surprised to see that I wasn't the angel, but had jeans on instead.

I opened the door, and it was just dark, nothing else.

So I put in a porno and sat back on my bed. I don't even remember the trick to day ratio, but I'd definitely been a horny boy. I don't know if I was horny so much, or I just knew that I couldn't get hard, and it just made me want to fuck like a dirty dog, because I knew I couldn't. It made me wish I could afford both speed and Viagra, but then I thought about this porn star that I started calling Lance Pounder. I don't know his real name, or even his porn name. (I skip the credits because they make me cum before the movie starts, and it sucks to be bored watching porn.) I just like watching the way Lance takes charge, pushing guys here and there until they're exposed and vulnerable. I wouldn't even care if he were looking out for my safety, as long as he owned me. As long as all the responsibility for me being who I am comes back to rest in his arms.

In perfect synchronization with Lance, there was a pounding at the window. I thought it was weird, like a sitcom rendition of Romeo and Juliet or something. It did remind me to check the TV listings, to see what's on later, because now and then, I do need a break from Lance Pounding. There's nothing on except the Golden Girls, and that short sassy one gives me the creeps. Just like that old man. Maybe he was lost in a senile daze and came knocking at my window. If I opened the blinds with a compulsive slowness, the light of the room would spill out onto his crazy eye. And the light would know where to go. It wouldn't light anything else, not a potted flower or a single blade of grass. It would just be drawn to his eye. Those things, things of horror, they're after my space, they want to invade me, and wear me like a suit. They are things of horror trying to take me down from the inside, but I won't let that happen.

So I filter back through all my thoughts of cops and landlords, and the amplifying powers of smoke. Once I see myself as the angel, I know it's OK to open the window. And I do, but then I think I bounced through too many thoughts of bathrobes and bed sheets or I was stuck in a Greek paradox where my mind was only moving, but the things around me did too or something. Fuck! I forget. I don't know why, but I just need to explain to myself why I heard the knocking so distinctly, yet there was only darkness, the same cracked sidewalk, a porch light and the pea green color of the apartment, and nothing more.

So I stood still like a predator, waiting for the thing that haunted me. I flattened myself up against the wall, next to the window, and waited to pounce. My skin faded to match the white of the wall, and my own features became indistinct bits of texture. I monitored my breathing to keep it slow enough to avoid detection. I counted my breaths while timing their duration. And then came the only sound in the world that hadn't become a part of me, and I jumped, ripping down the shade and there he is, an angelic face in a baseball cap, or perhaps my downfall.

I open the window, and he asks if I'm still looking to hook up. I do a lot of cruising on the phone lines, and the internet, but I don't remember inviting anybody over, so I'm suspicious. He could be anybody. I have to keep an eye on him. He may know my darkest secrets or my landlord. He's an agent of the man with the crazy eye! Damn! Why am I remembering so much with a spy in the room trying to make his way into my head. I'll play it so cool, he'll think I'm just any old phone trick. I'll show him.

"Come around to the door and I'll suck your dick".

I walked him to the bed, and remembered that the cat pissed there a few days ago, but it's got to be dry by now. I let her outside after that. Shit! He probably can't smell it anyway with all the smoke in the room. He pulls his pants down just far enough for business, and I play along. By the time I look up the porno is over. I lost track of time, I guess. I do get into sucking cock, and spy or not, he has a nice one. I started to get nervous, because he hadn't come. He didn't reach down to jerk himself or anything. He was enjoying it. He was just watching, trying to decode my performance to see the anxiety I kept so well hidden. He knows that the longer it takes, the weaker I'll get. And then I heard the knocking. It wasn't the door or the window, the landlord or this guy's beating heart. It was coming from the floorboards, and he just sat there with his hands behind his head, eyes closed, and a smug smile. I could hear the old man's beating heart and that sound, coupled with my horror soothed this sick fucker.

So I bit him. I know he is bleeding because I can taste it. But before he can scream , I am already at the closet, grabbing a crowbar. "Tear up the floor boards; you'll find the old man there".

Part Three

I can feel the tumor in my chest. I know its position. It presses my ribs near the sternum and I can feel its depth. I know how far it presses into my lungs, and how hard it pushes against the bones. I get a perfect image of its shape as it spreads between organs. I can imagine the black pustule, feeding from my veins. My beating heart feeds the disease. It's insides are just as soft and silky pink as my own. It just has more yellow-green, that hue that never signifies beauty.

A doctor might tell me I've got a year to live. No more than a year. But that seems like enough. I know time escapes me, but I'm not doing so much. I've never found my thing. I looked for meaning in the usual places: art, love, poetry, medicine, invention, religion. They all came up empty. Just empty. And so I wonder what I am if the external world fails. How can I be about nothing, because if I'm not defined, what am I? So yes, a year in this body seems like plenty.

I understand the body's propensity to self regulate. I've learned how to interpret the systems that keep my body running. I know the warning signs. They come up like red lights on the dashboard. I can't deny a single craving, because my body tells me what I need. I can quantify disease to determine how long a fever will last. I just have to pause myself until I am so still I can hear in my heart the harsh revving of a machine. I can feel the flow of blood in the tiniest capillaries. I analyze my body's chemistry, determine deficiencies and restore the balance.

I'm scared in a way that doesn't allow me to plan for the future. I don't know how to spend the days. What can I make myself into? What kind of person do I want to be when I die?

It feels like pop rocks under my skin, or maybe the bubbles in soda that shoot above the rim of the glass. Maybe they've just joined into a fatal combination. The feeling is a distinct fizzle. Nothing hits a nerve, so I don't cry out. There's no pain, just the tingling knowledge of a disease. It's just the feeling of tiny fibers in my muscles giving way, being pushed aside by a malignant growth. It's just below the skin, I can feel it pressing up against the roots of hairs, and pushing down through the muscles.

We understand life by the potential for death, but it's another thing to feel it happening. Mortality is no longer an abstract; it's shifted from its place in the shadows. It's no longer darkness, but a distant illumination. But still there's nothing waiting for me. The light on the other side is just an empty promise of warmth.

I spent a half hour grieving. I didn't have to look at the clock. On my back, tears tickled my cheeks, then my ears. I tried to understand the effect of my death among family and friends. My mother's sense of the world was bound up in my smile. I guess her dreams will be gone, though it's more to do with her than me. I can see my father's smug expression. He doesn't yet know how haunting victory can be. My sister doesn't understand. She doesn't understand change. It's just that my number will be disconnected and there will be no replacement. I think she's afraid of pragmatism. Smaller changes have sent her into violent rages. I feel sorry for her dog.

It all made sense in a heady rush. I understood the tumor. I remembered how often he cooked for me, the dark bottle on the counter. He said it was gin, but there wasn't a label. Then that damn missing water bill. And the messes he leaves in the living room. He thinks he can drive me crazy. He's poisoning me and he thinks I won't even notice the toxins taking me down. He thinks I'll just succumb, without a word, without a thought. And he's sleeping so soundly next to me, the pleasure in his face as he enjoys a fucking dream.

He's using something like arsenic, something that builds up over time, but it can't be so conventional. He's not a risk taker. And he's smarter than that. He must have involved a chemist. It has to be something new, specific and undetectable. I'm not even going to make it through the night. I'll never get to tell my story. Nobody will ever know. I'll just be another sheet of concrete in a procession of monuments built to allow forgetting. I just don't know where to start. I've become too weak to crawl to the bathroom, yet I have this reserve of anger. So I'll rest, still like a spider, waiting for the springs to move. When I feel his gentle pulsing through the mattress, I'll pounce. I'll grab him by the throat. My two thumbs should have just enough pressure to take him with me.

Part Four

The scenes of Goya are gouged and smeared at the bottom of the door. It's all smoke and limbs. Nature isn't even left standing. Just the door.

Peacock Feathers

after Arthur Silver

Each morning she left the constricting comfort of the forest canopy and caught the bus to Antarctica. She threaded the laces into her black veined, dingy vinyl high-tops, strings frayed, about to snap. She imagined herself as a bearded explorer, her yellowed white shirt and faded black pants became furs insulated with walrus blubber. Instead of the crumpled brown lunch bag, she carried a weather worn oak tripod that would stabilize the instrument that would take the measurement that would reveal a minor secret about the desolate land of penguin and caribou that would influence the final understanding of what it's all about.

She'd never really been to the underside of the earth, but decided the frozen continent looked a lot like the inside of a freezer, bulging structures of loose packed crystals, long nights and murky grays, infrequent flashes of daylight. It was a continent defined by unknown monuments, crystalline and shady. The Antarctic ice plateaus would occasionally offer the surprise of a sparkle, but so did the stone surface of the building she worked in.

She didn't understand how a continent, a space much larger than the edges of everything she knew could be kept frozen for hundreds of years. A long summer heat should melt anything, she felt certain. And if the sun didn't melt it all away each year, then the ice age must be creeping ever so slowly toward her, and she was afraid of frostbite, haunted by the image of Jack Nicholson at the end of The Shining—even the blanket was frozen stiff. An incredible ridge of mountains contained the shores of the continent, held in the cold, blocked out the sun, kept the white animal inhabitants in the dark chill they understood. That's the only way it could work.

She was familiar with ice crystals; they were harder than light. Somewhere between the speed of a Ford and a jet plane was the speed of light. At this pace photons would travel from sun or star, and fracture as they struck a cold and rigid body of ice. White light was transformed into ricocheted glints of grayish blue and dull magenta. She saw these same colors break off of flecks embedded in the surface of architecture. She knew that the stones had a special relationship to ice, quarried in the cold, or perhaps it was something more sinister. The freeze-box was a model for a world that had no relationship to anything she knew, except maybe some half forgotten memory of a claymation Christmas program: low resolution movements with brightly colored accents.

Antarctica: the north pole, a blanket of snow walled in by a collection of giant ice chunks dotted with white fur and red pointed hats, each tipped by a single golden bell and worn by an elf whose thick, calloused feet were filled with blubber and jiggled awkwardly, making them unsteady on their feet. The hearts of the elves raced at three times the rate of a human pulse; the rapid flow of blood prevented freezing.

Icebergs and skyscrapers were just huge, bright monoliths that conspired against nature, rejecting the sun's heat. On the brightest days those tall buildings remained cold and damp. On the hottest days of summer, in the heart of weeklong heat waves, if she leaned against the stone surface of an office building while waiting for her bus, she'd freeze until she shivered. The moisture in the air collected in her clothes, passed through her skin and settled inside her bones–focused on her knees.

In an intense freeze constructed in a laboratory to achieve the temperature of deep space, thick steel blocks were shattered with a gentle tap. The cold makes things brittle. Solid steel bars behaved like candy canes and chicken bones. She felt that same deep freeze accumulating in her knees as she walked to the bus to the city. The chill met her after work and followed her home at night. Just by leaning against a building her blood was infected by an agent, an enemy of the sun. Solar rays would fail to warm her after an exposure to the pathogen of the cold. She could see the light bend, leaving her in slight shadow, so she was a little darker, a little hazier than others. This thin aurora flashed against her immediate space, disturbed the image of things very close to her, structures wavered in the warped light, text blurred on its page.

The cold focused the freeze at the center of the meal or marrow, chilling from the inside out. As she walked, she worried that the bones in her knees were chipping away at each other. Each step felt grittier than the one before. She walked with the understanding that her joints were slowly sharpening the blunt stumps of her bones. She knew that one day they would jump their sockets, gouging their way into the light of the world.

There was no reprieve in an afterlife, only removal, a complete deceleration within a wordless space. There were no more pictures to collect, just a black stop.

Occasionally, at work she felt soothed. When her head buzzed along with the ambient noise of the kitchen, she could lose herself in the totality of it all. The steam of the dishwasher made her sweat and the earthy textures of sauce smeared across the white face of a plate gave the sensations of art. Her mind was moved beyond the itch of a rolling sweat drop and the smell of mustard diluted in bleach. There was a strange freedom in that moment, perspiration, fatigue, it was what people pretend to get from sex or might get from drugs or surely find in death.

Only a single pan hung from the scratched and yellowing white plastic rack in her own kitchen. The cracked black bottom of the pan showed a silver web of tin beneath the burnt crust, and its tan exterior walls matched the grease covering the rest of the kitchen. She kept a shelf of owls there as well. One day, her grandmother asked what she collected. She was startled by the question, so trivial, but presented with such gravity. Her main passion had been collecting handkerchiefs left unattended by the neighbor's handyman. She didn't know his name but knew that admitting these petty thefts wouldn't satisfy her grandmother. She'd seen racks of figurines in most homes, but she never wondered what sort of nick-knacks would one day compose miniature scenes along her own walls. Her grandmother said that everybody collects something: geese, pigs, frogs. Its how a woman makes her own space in his home, how she marks a space to retreat. A man's collection consisted of beer cans and ammunition.

At age 13, she was asked to define herself, to pick something that would forever be associated with her, an inalienable quality that would highlight both Christmas and Birthdays. "Owls." It was said, forever in an instant. This strange scene with her grandmother had the same awkward pressure as a marriage proposal, though perhaps more intense, because marriage offers the possibility of divorce.

Her collection of ceramic, stuffed, google eyed and head bobbing owls arrived in semiannual installments from up and down the family tree. With the arrival of each new piece, she carefully covered her resentment with hugs and thanks. It eliminated the pretense of pretending to know her. Perfect social relations involved finding an owl whose price reflected personal interest and delivering it on an appropriate day. Yet there they were so many wide eyes staring, long after her grandmother died, after she cut contact with her mother, so many addresses since the last Christmas card, so long since she thought about herself.

The porcelain shapes collected a fuzzy dust over the suffocating layer of grease. The nap of the cloth toys clumped into spikes, stained by the kitchen air. But this was it, the kitchen, it's where she worked, what she came home to. The water in her home never got
as hot as the steam that constantly wafted in her face as she raised and lowered the stainless door of the dishwasher. The cracks in the sink, the path worn into ancient linoleum, the once white walls told her that everything was OK.

Her occasional boyfriends sat at the table she rescued from the garbage during a remodel of a restaurant two jobs before. It was a printed plastic veneer covered with sputnik dingbats in both robins egg and gold. It was obviously a restaurant table, supported by a central pole nailed to the floor. The base was supposed to be covered by a chrome plate, but that had been either lost or mangled. After installation, she scrubbed the table top with a green pad and an abrasive cleaner until most of the print had worn white. She tried to scrub away the angled letters that had been gouged by a midnight customer with a dripping steak knife. She had no luck. All her guests would know immediately that "DEBBIE SUX".

Men usually asked who Debbie was, and then she'd feel pressure to live up to the reputation or allegation. On her knees, under the table, her ass would hit the support column and her head would rock the table top. She sucked diligently but without inspiration at some version of cock, while the usually bearded, usually pot-bellied, smelly drunk or junkie picked through the mess of hamburger and noodles on his plate. Most guys wondered if her son ever walked in on these scenes, and if he did was it a turn on or off.

She didn't enjoy these episodes, but they were a means to an end, so she didn't necessarily mind. Sucking dick kept her from talking, and the less she spoke, the longer they stayed. If she opened up, they'd call her a crazy bitch, so she saved her thoughts for the break-up, when she was ready to be pushed from the car, ready for that crestfallen walk back to solitude.

She had theories. Science and paranoia achieved tentative cohesion inside her head. She had difficulty understanding conversations, but she could hear the syllables and repeat them, provide approximate meanings for individual words. In groups, the sounds were more slippery. Language was a scattered mess of colors that were too abstract to function. The bumpy bus route into town always made her think of words, jumbled by the force of the ride.

When there were no men around, photons and molecules were the invading forces that presented the greatest challenge to her daily happiness. The government, minor players—not much cause for concern. Their function was concealment, but she didn't care, since she'd pierced the veil, stared straight into the machinations of reality, experienced the burn. It was the feeling represented by a frame of celluloid melting in a projector, and could only be explained to a certain point. In a lucid but half dreaming state, she came to understand that her difficulties with language came from years of exposure to fry grease, having worked so many years in kitchens. The molecules that compose the sound of a human voice, those specialized particles, combinations of oxygenated potassium and nitrates that represent every sound in all languages, are interpreted by the ear, become coated with a thin film of grease as they are pushed from the breath into the ear of a kitchen worker. That's earwax. If the wax isn't cleaned frequently enough, and there's no way for a dishwasher to keep up, it melts from the heat of the room and slides around the brain. The passageway for the word molecules gets coated with grease, so that all words entering her ear pick up a bit of the lubricant, slip and slide within her mind. That's why she couldn't hold a thought. That's why she needed a man, to keep straight the jumble inside her head.

Women leave after being hit, because it means they've found the limits of a man, moved him beyond the flat emotional tones of masculinity, drained him of power and reduced him to a laughable lump, covering his head in the back of a squad car. Violence escalates. Women know when composure will fail, the impenetrable and cold faÂade cracks against the shrill sting of a woman's laughter. She can see his explosion in her mind and determine his next step. A gesture of her head or hand, the flick of a tongue or the twist of a curl—she decides if he'll put the fury in to her cunt or against a wall. They want blood either way. Will he bite her tongue, neck and cheeks, or will she call him a failure, an impotent cocksucker as she blocks her face? From that semi-protected view, peeking out from between her arms, she overcomes him. Crashing dishes, broken sheetrock, pets or chairs, a sublime wonder. She made the scene and takes the credit, satisfaction in the back of her mind.

She couldn't keep track of her son. He was wherever he happened to be and she couldn't remember it any other way. He was too much for her to keep straight. He loved to roam, and she thought exploration was a good skill to develop, perhaps there's another continent to be discovered. He built his own shelter, occupied himself. He was a vagabond constrained by a thin emotional connection to home. He would eat there while she was asleep or away. She knew because of the food scraps, the crumbs that were mashed between floorboards, a scrap of crust that moved from the garbage to the floor or an extra notch in the cutting board. She wouldn't see him for months, then just glances of a fleeting figure through the distance and the trees. But the minute details or rearrangements in her kitchen revealed his proximity and safety. The nuances of the change were too fine to be the work of a 'possum.

The television rang out announcing the shots. There was speculation of terrorism. Nobody knew. An apparent nobody was shot from apparently nowhere. A citizen, average in all respects. The police said the who and why were still very far away. The most pressing questions had the most distant answers. But when she saw the delicate architecture of the victim's blonde hair, the lumps that composed her middle age figure, the generic blue Japanese economy car, she knew it was him. She knew her baby hadn't just disappeared, but found his way.

She was more proud than the day she tried to find him, the day she found his curtained copse in the forest behind the house. The light filtered inside through a fine network of limbs that approximated a rotunda, and cut the light into a haze of rays. The doorway was a blanket, granny squares that her mother brought once on a visit, so many years ago. It glowed, and she began to understand the design of the place. It was a cathedral that provided the lessons of life and death that she had failed to provide.

The atmosphere had the stink of mildew, etc. It smelled as much like rotting
leaves as rotting flesh. She looked down: a corner with a filthy sleeping bag folded open, leaves crunched inside of it. His skin cells had been scraped on the edges of pieces of dried fragments of leaves, so she collected them in her hand. No pillow. Most of the floor was covered with cardboard that was wet, dense and had started to merge into the dirt. The place was strewn with pieces of broken machines, broken birds.

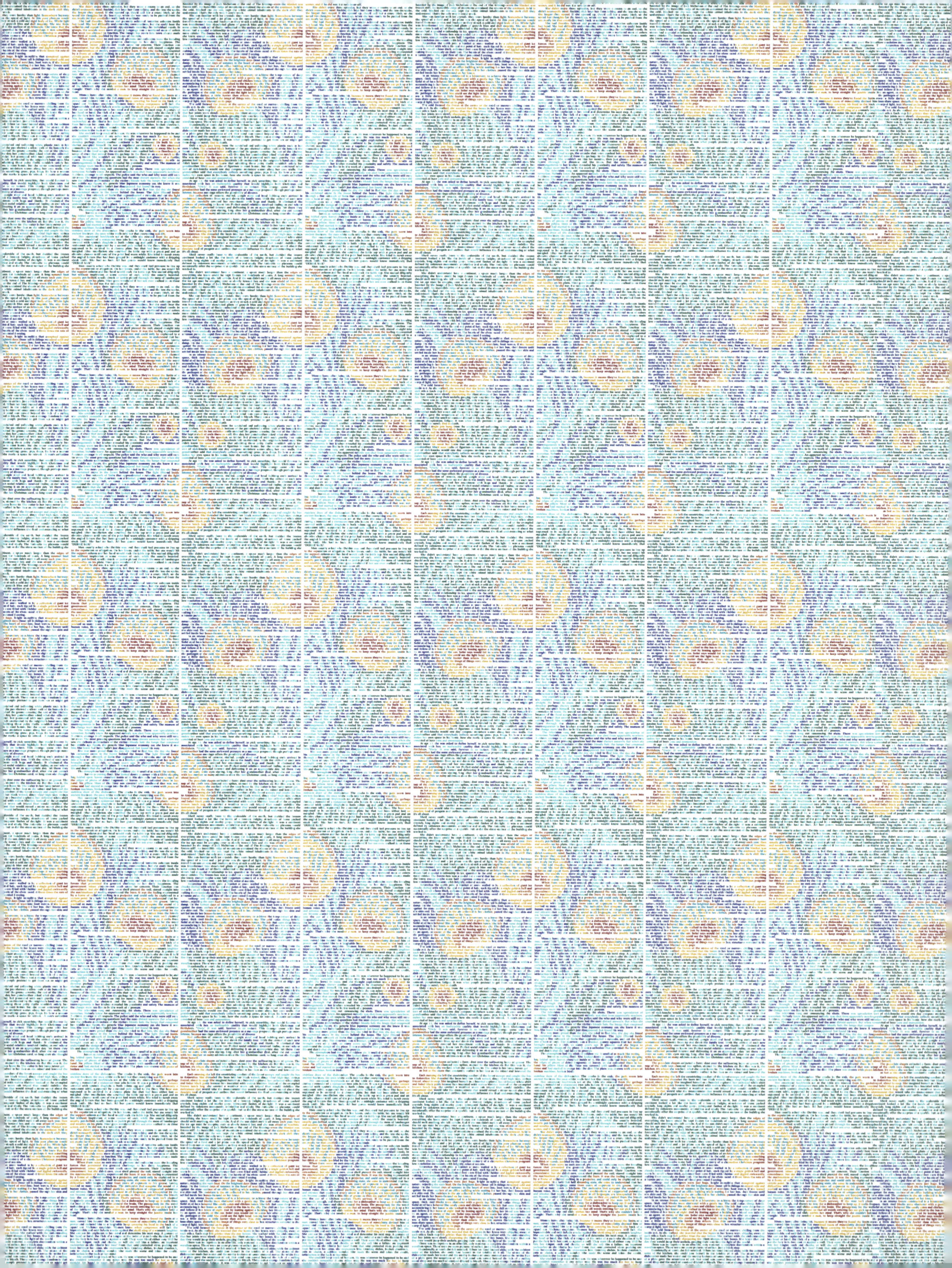

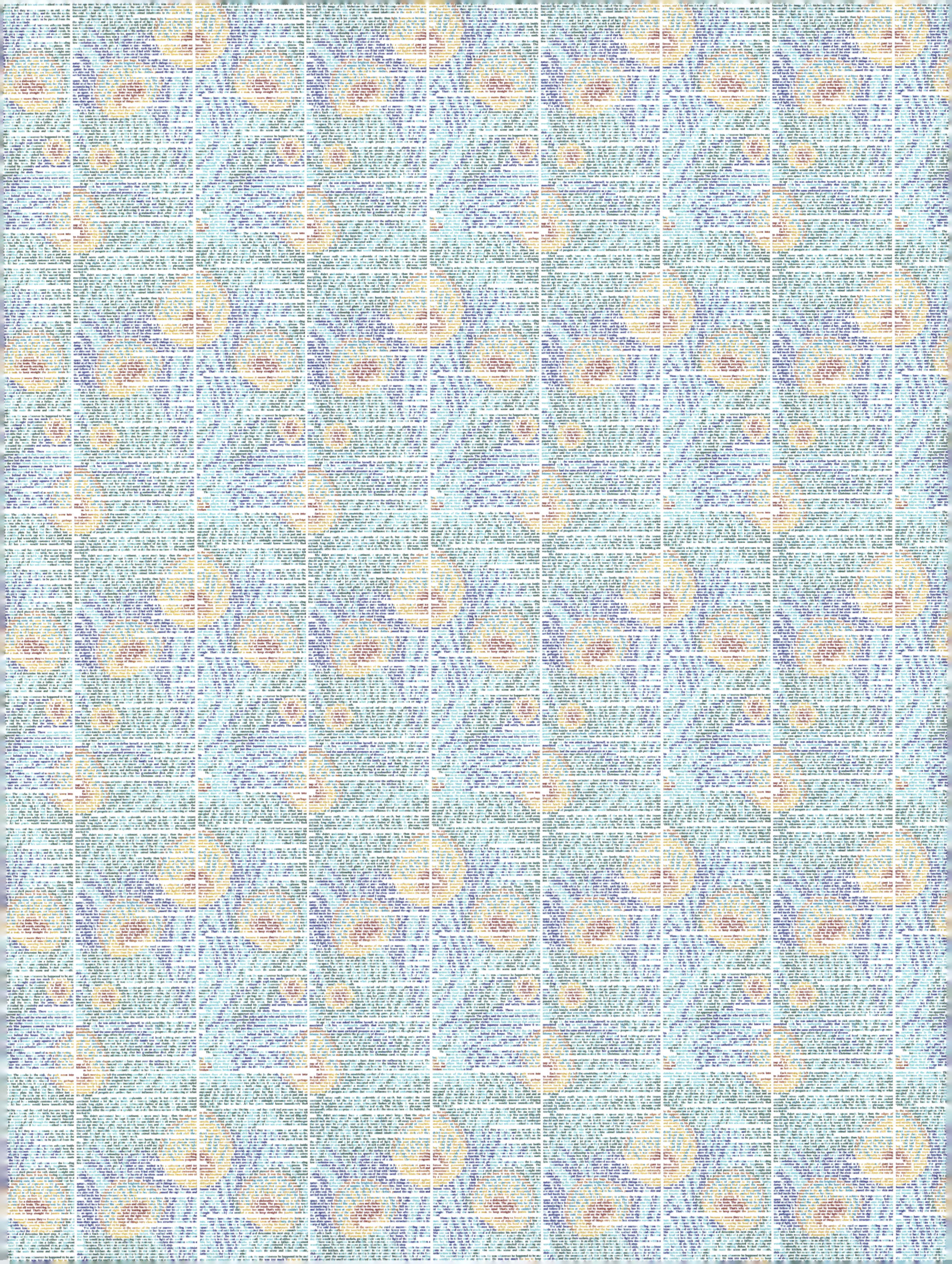

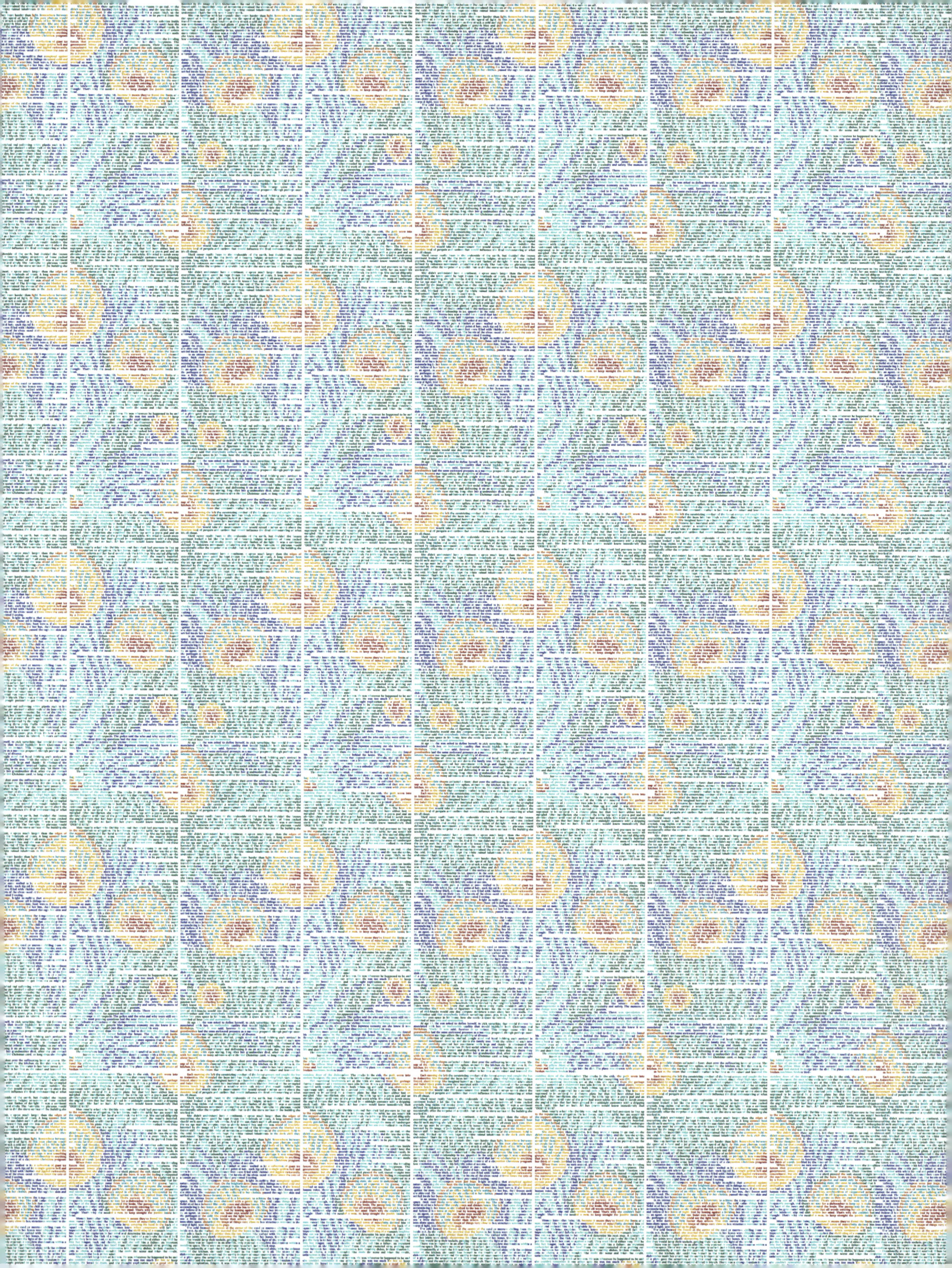

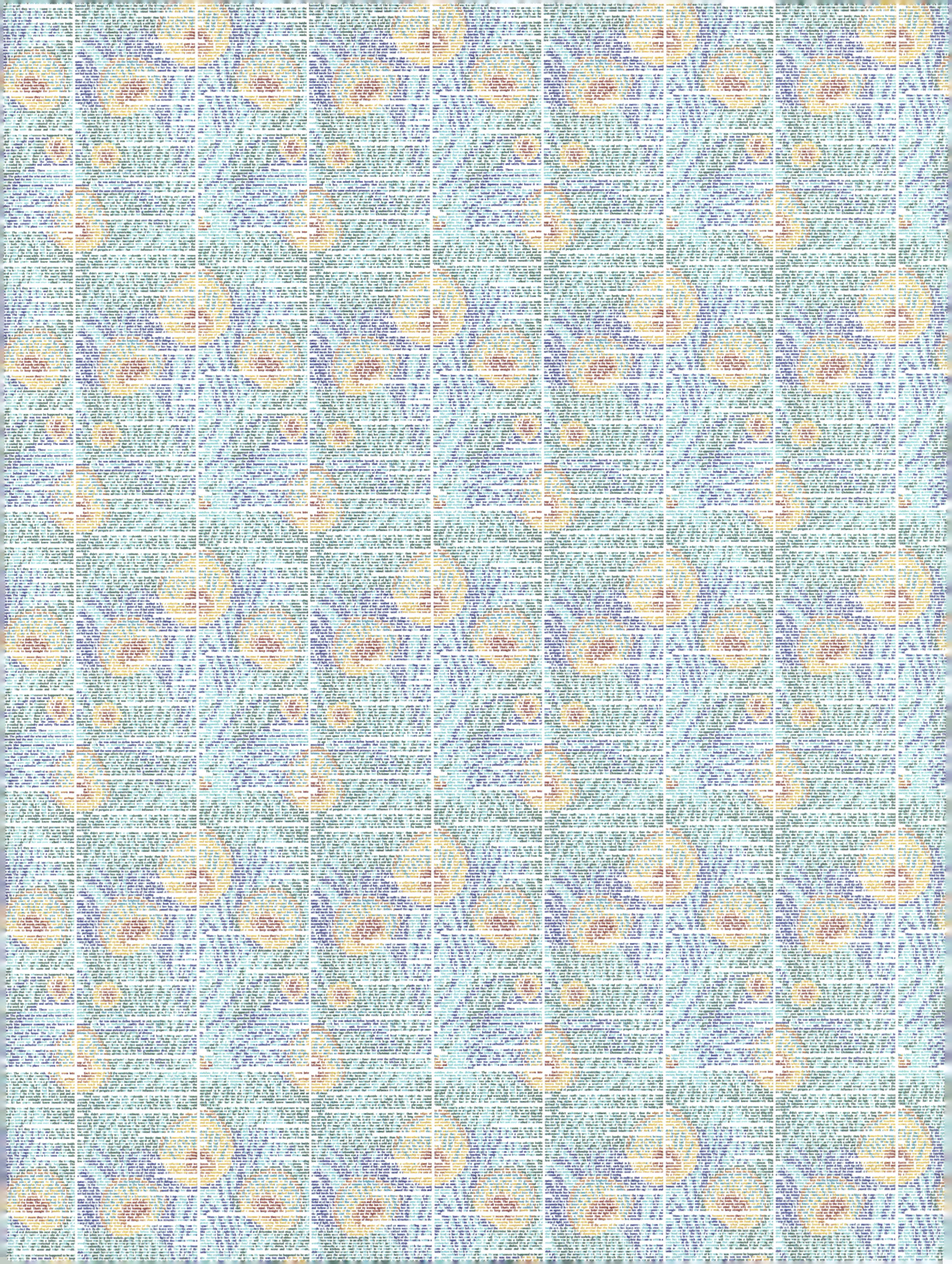

Each morning she left the constricting comfort of the forest canopy and caught the bus to Antarctica. She threaded the laces into her black veined, dingy vinyl high-tops, strings frayed, about to snap. She imagined herself as a bearded explorer, her yellowed white shirt and faded black pants became furs insulated with walrus blubber. Instead of the crumpled brown lunch bag, she carried a weather worn oak tripod that would stabilize the instrument that would take the measurement that would reveal a minor secret about the desolate land of penguin and caribou that would influence the final understanding of what it's all about.

She'd never really been to the underside of the earth, but decided the frozen continent looked a lot like the inside of a freezer, bulging structures of loose packed crystals, long nights and murky grays, infrequent flashes of daylight. It was a continent defined by unknown monuments, crystalline and shady. The Antarctic ice plateaus would occasionally offer the surprise of a sparkle, but so did the stone surface of the building she worked in.

She didn't understand how a continent, a space much larger than the edges of everything she knew could be kept frozen for hundreds of years. A long summer heat should melt anything, she felt certain. And if the sun didn't melt it all away each year, then the ice age must be creeping ever so slowly toward her, and she was afraid of frostbite, haunted by the image of Jack Nicholson at the end of The Shining—even the blanket was frozen stiff. An incredible ridge of mountains contained the shores of the continent, held in the cold, blocked out the sun, kept the white animal inhabitants in the dark chill they understood. That's the only way it could work.

She was familiar with ice crystals; they were harder than light. Somewhere between the speed of a Ford and a jet plane was the speed of light. At this pace photons would travel from sun or star, and fracture as they struck a cold and rigid body of ice. White light was transformed into ricocheted glints of grayish blue and dull magenta. She saw these same colors break off of flecks embedded in the surface of architecture. She knew that the stones had a special relationship to ice, quarried in the cold, or perhaps it was something more sinister. The freeze-box was a model for a world that had no relationship to anything she knew, except maybe some half forgotten memory of a claymation Christmas program: low resolution movements with brightly colored accents.

Antarctica: the north pole, a blanket of snow walled in by a collection of giant ice chunks dotted with white fur and red pointed hats, each tipped by a single golden bell and worn by an elf whose thick, calloused feet were filled with blubber and jiggled awkwardly, making them unsteady on their feet. The hearts of the elves raced at three times the rate of a human pulse; the rapid flow of blood prevented freezing.

Icebergs and skyscrapers were just huge, bright monoliths that conspired against nature, rejecting the sun's heat. On the brightest days those tall buildings remained cold and damp. On the hottest days of summer, in the heart of weeklong heat waves, if she leaned against the stone surface of an office building while waiting for her bus, she'd freeze until she shivered. The moisture in the air collected in her clothes, passed through her skin and settled inside her bones–focused on her knees.

In an intense freeze constructed in a laboratory to achieve the temperature of deep space, thick steel blocks were shattered with a gentle tap. The cold makes things brittle. Solid steel bars behaved like candy canes and chicken bones. She felt that same deep freeze accumulating in her knees as she walked to the bus to the city. The chill met her after work and followed her home at night. Just by leaning against a building her blood was infected by an agent, an enemy of the sun. Solar rays would fail to warm her after an exposure to the pathogen of the cold. She could see the light bend, leaving her in slight shadow, so she was a little darker, a little hazier than others. This thin aurora flashed against her immediate space, disturbed the image of things very close to her, structures wavered in the warped light, text blurred on its page.

The cold focused the freeze at the center of the meal or marrow, chilling from the inside out. As she walked, she worried that the bones in her knees were chipping away at each other. Each step felt grittier than the one before. She walked with the understanding that her joints were slowly sharpening the blunt stumps of her bones. She knew that one day they would jump their sockets, gouging their way into the light of the world.

There was no reprieve in an afterlife, only removal, a complete deceleration within a wordless space. There were no more pictures to collect, just a black stop.

Occasionally, at work she felt soothed. When her head buzzed along with the ambient noise of the kitchen, she could lose herself in the totality of it all. The steam of the dishwasher made her sweat and the earthy textures of sauce smeared across the white face of a plate gave the sensations of art. Her mind was moved beyond the itch of a rolling sweat drop and the smell of mustard diluted in bleach. There was a strange freedom in that moment, perspiration, fatigue, it was what people pretend to get from sex or might get from drugs or surely find in death.

Only a single pan hung from the scratched and yellowing white plastic rack in her own kitchen. The cracked black bottom of the pan showed a silver web of tin beneath the burnt crust, and its tan exterior walls matched the grease covering the rest of the kitchen. She kept a shelf of owls there as well. One day, her grandmother asked what she collected. She was startled by the question, so trivial, but presented with such gravity. Her main passion had been collecting handkerchiefs left unattended by the neighbor's handyman. She didn't know his name but knew that admitting these petty thefts wouldn't satisfy her grandmother. She'd seen racks of figurines in most homes, but she never wondered what sort of nick-knacks would one day compose miniature scenes along her own walls. Her grandmother said that everybody collects something: geese, pigs, frogs. Its how a woman makes her own space in his home, how she marks a space to retreat. A man's collection consisted of beer cans and ammunition.

At age 13, she was asked to define herself, to pick something that would forever be associated with her, an inalienable quality that would highlight both Christmas and Birthdays. "Owls." It was said, forever in an instant. This strange scene with her grandmother had the same awkward pressure as a marriage proposal, though perhaps more intense, because marriage offers the possibility of divorce.

Her collection of ceramic, stuffed, google eyed and head bobbing owls arrived in semiannual installments from up and down the family tree. With the arrival of each new piece, she carefully covered her resentment with hugs and thanks. It eliminated the pretense of pretending to know her. Perfect social relations involved finding an owl whose price reflected personal interest and delivering it on an appropriate day. Yet there they were, so many wide eyes staring, long after her grandmother died, after she cut contact with her mother, so many addresses since the last Christmas card, so long since she thought about herself.

The porcelain shapes collected a fuzzy dust over the suffocating layer of grease. The nap of the cloth toys clumped into spikes, stained by the kitchen air. But this was it, the kitchen, it's where she worked, what she came home to. The water in her home never got as hot as the steam that constantly wafted in her face as she raised and lowered the stainless door of the dishwasher. The cracks in the sink, the path worn into ancient linoleum, the once white walls told her that everything was OK.

Her occasional boyfriends sat at the table she rescued from the garbage during a remodel of a restaurant two jobs before. It was a printed plastic veneer covered with sputnik dingbats in both robins egg and gold. It was obviously a restaurant table, supported by a central pole nailed to the floor. The base was supposed to be covered by a chrome plate, but that had been either lost or mangled. After installation, she scrubbed the table top with a green pad and an abrasive cleaner until most of the print had worn white. She tried to scrub away the angled letters that had been gouged by a midnight customer with a dripping steak knife. She had no luck. All her guests would know immediately that "DEBBIE SUX".

Men usually asked who Debbie was, and then she'd feel pressure to live up to the reputation or allegation. On her knees, under the table, her ass would hit the support column and her head would rock the table top. She sucked diligently but without inspiration at some version of cock, while the usually bearded, usually pot-bellied, smelly drunk or junkie picked through the mess of hamburger and noodles on his plate. Most guys wondered if her son ever walked in on these scenes, and if he did was it a turn on or off.

She didn't enjoy these episodes, but they were a means to an end, so she didn't necessarily mind. Sucking dick kept her from talking, and the less she spoke, the longer they stayed. If she opened up, they'd call her a crazy bitch, so she saved her thoughts for the break-up, when she was ready to be pushed from the car, ready for that crestfallen walk back to solitude.

She had theories. Science and paranoia achieved tentative cohesion inside her head. She had difficulty understanding conversations, but she could hear the syllables and repeat them, provide approximate meanings for individual words. In groups, the sounds were more slippery. Language was a scattered mess of colors that were too abstract to function. The bumpy bus route into town always made her think of words, jumbled by the force of the ride.

When there were no men around, photons and molecules were the invading forces that presented the greatest challenge to her daily happiness. The government, minor players—not much cause for concern. Their function was concealment, but she didn't care, since she'd pierced the veil, stared straight into the machinations of reality, experienced the burn. It was the feeling represented by a frame of celluloid melting in a projector, and could only be explained to a certain point. In a lucid but half dreaming state, she came to understand that her difficulties with language came from years of exposure to fry grease, having worked so many years in kitchens. The molecules that compose the sound of a human voice, those specialized particles, combinations of oxygenated potassium and nitrates that represent every sound in all languages, are interpreted by the ear, become coated with a thin film of grease as they are pushed from the breath into the ear of a kitchen worker. That's earwax. If the wax isn't cleaned frequently enough, and there's no way for a dishwasher to keep up, it melts from the heat of the room and slides around the brain. The passageway for the word molecules gets coated with grease, so that all words entering her ear pick up a bit of the lubricant, slip and slide within her mind. That's why she couldn't hold a thought. That's why she needed a man, to keep straight the jumble inside her head.

Women leave after being hit, because it means they've found the limits of a man, moved him beyond the flat emotional tones of masculinity, drained him of power and reduced him to a laughable lump, covering his head in the back of a squad car. Violence escalates. Women know when composure will fail, the impenetrable and cold facade cracks against the shrill sting of a woman's laughter. She can see his explosion in her mind and determine his next step. A gesture of her head or hand, the flick of a tongue or the twist of a curl—she decides if he'll put the fury in to her cunt or against a wall. They want blood either way. Will he bite her tongue, neck and cheeks, or will she call him a failure, an impotent cocksucker as she blocks her face? From that semi-protected view, peeking out from between her arms, she overcomes him. Crashing dishes, broken sheetrock, pets or chairs, a sublime wonder. She made the scene and takes the credit, satisfaction in the back of her mind.

She couldn't keep track of her son. He was wherever he happened to be and she couldn't remember it any other way. He was too much for her to keep straight. He loved to roam, and she thought exploration was a good skill to develop, perhaps there's another continent to be discovered. He built his own shelter, occupied himself. He was a vagabond constrained by a thin emotional connection to home. He would eat there while she was asleep or away. She knew because of the food scraps, the crumbs that were mashed between floorboards, a scrap of crust that moved from the garbage to the floor or an extra notch in the cutting board. She wouldn't see him for months, then just glances of a fleeting figure through the distance and the trees. But the minute details or rearrangements in her kitchen revealed his proximity and safety. The nuances of the change were too fine to be the work of a 'possum.

The television rang out announcing the shots. There was speculation of terrorism. Nobody knew. An apparent nobody was shot from apparently nowhere. A citizen, average in all respects. The police said the who and why were still very far away. The most pressing questions had the most distant answers. But when she saw the delicate architecture of the victim's blonde hair, the lumps that composed her middle age figure, the generic blue Japanese economy car, she knew it was him. She knew her baby hadn't just disappeared, but found his way.

She was more proud than the day she tried to find him, the day she found his curtained copse in the forest behind the house. The light filtered inside through a fine network of limbs that approximated a rotunda, and cut the light into a haze of rays. The doorway was a blanket, granny squares that her mother brought once on a visit, so many years ago. It glowed, and she began to understand the design of the place. It was a cathedral that provided the lessons of life and death that she had failed to provide.

The atmosphere had the stink of mildew, etc. It smelled as much like rotting leaves as rotting flesh. She looked down: a corner with a filthy sleeping bag folded open, leaves crunched inside of it. His skin cells had been scraped on the edges of pieces of dried fragments of leaves, so she collected them in her hand. No pillow. Most of the floor was covered with cardboard that was wet, dense and had started to merge into the dirt. The place was strewn with pieces of broken machines, broken birds.

Trellis
after William Morris

With the exception of crank labs that explode vertically, blowing a charred hole through layers of sagging shingle and leaving the exterior walls unscathed, it was difficult to tell which houses had been abandoned. There was a pervasive aesthetic of disrepair or disassemble. A missing door didn't mean empty, just broken. Broken down, broken in, a peeling veneer revealing the skeleton of a hollow core. Several families might live behind thin walls, protected only by an aluminum mesh over the entrance. Their pooled resources fed habits and naked children, covered a miniscule mortgage taken against the home, that meager inheritance. Dreams and speed don't come cheap.

Discerning decrepit from abandoned is a matter of connoisseurship. After people leave, the walls are the first to go. Kids don't start the destruction; they finish it. Kids don't understand that a house is a copper mine, and the junk of its guts gets traded for cash.

After pans and clothes are packed into the bed of an El Camino, under flashlight and moonlight, the house is open to all. The neighbors' friendly waving hands become the desperado's violent grasp: punching through plaster, pulling out wire. Wad it up, burn it up. The plastic housing melts away leaving pure salvage value in its place. Maybe 80 cents a pound.

Toilets, swag lamps, faucets and drawer pulls are currency, replacements for something broken, saved for a special occasion. Poverty is navigated with a stockpile of porcelain and pull-chains. Potential use, potential value, trash to trade in a time of need.

When kids come, windows break. It's an introduction to transgression, breaking a familial structure from a safe distance. The duration of a rock's flight through space allows plausible deniability, the warped reflection of total destruction.

Graffiti inscribes new values: loves and hates, cunts and fucks, lyrics for feelings, gypsum dust scraped into lines.

Bodies replace Barbies. Square haircuts and ink pen makeovers become the taste of tongue and sweat, the smells of crotch and jerky breath. Coke cans become beer cans, black label bottles among cigarette butts. Practicing addiction is a private affair; its public premier must be convincing. Growing up means learning tolerance, but still, no niggers allowed.

Front yards were junkyards and back yards were worse. The front yard held forgotten fruit trees, planted for sustenance by a depression era mother. Most remained small, withered. Only one was suitable for climbing. Debris piled around trees, the strewn remains of home improvement. A rusty lawnmower, poised to tackle the weeds that grew up through its wheels. A useless red wagon, leaning at one corner, its red body rinsed with rust. The metal became a jagged filigree mapping an assortment of lost continents. Traffic and neglect had yellowed the path to a patch of lawn covered with misshapen swatches of found carpet, quilted dirt for children to play on. It wasn't the useful rectangle of organized sport, but the shape of cancer and the color of cartoons, encroached by filth, hemmed in by a ditch. On the porch, dozens of plants in crumbling terra cotta. Potted landscape surrounded the ass end of a leaky swamp cooler protruding from a window. Kitten's Ear, Spider Plant, Martians' Toes, browning from neglect, but still a mother's finest passion.

In a dusty side yard sat a Chevy Citation, red where it wasn't primer grey, a white hood and no wheels. It wasn't preserved on jacks, so it sank to the fenders, slowly claimed by winters' mud. A convertible Fiat missing its top, sat under a cover that sagged into the cab, full of rain, dirt and rotting leaves.

On the porch, boxes of miscellanea, clothes and screws, Greasy rubber seals and romance novels, knick-knacks and porno mags all mingled in molding cardboard. Fruits fell from the large tree, the one that survived against total neglect. Mulberries smashed into the driveway, smeared under the tread of late night visitors. A grotesque brown film covered the cement and an alcoholic smell invaded the house. Cars slid to a stop over the mess of pulp and seed. But nobody ever tried to clean it up; winter rains washed the mess away.

The back yard was divided by a ramshackle building, an adult-sized hideout, built over the remains of a garden. Three cars lined the flaccid fence from the gate to the sagging sliding garage door. Cars were parked to resemble order: an Impala whose front end was a smashed black cavity without an engine, a Corvair missing a transmission, a pile of pieces, Camaro and/or Bel Aire. Dream cars in nightmare condition, collected for restoration, a quick buck off an allegedly meager task. Poor investment machinery. They rested under the canopy of pecan trees, among leaves piled thick, stifling the weeds that weren't already stunted by the seepage of oil and battery acid.

Behind the shop, garage, adult playroom or fire hazard, was a large unused space of yard. Raspberries were once grown there, harvested and sold at the local market. But the bushes were burnt, and that part of the yard was left fallow. Overgrown, green became yellow during summer droughts. A lone vine survived the scorch. At the farthest end was a pile of rubble, walls of broken concrete arranged in a circle holding a heaping mound of garbage.

The backyard was off limits. The patriarch built his skull and bones, his degenerate clubhouse, a grown-up fort made with scraps culled from construction site dumpsters. Blue tarp roof, no windows, total privacy, secrecy within the patchwork of plywood. Stained, dusty wooden crates lined the walls, filled with the clunky greasy parts of cars, a prodigious collection of screws, nuts and bolts, a rolling metal chest of tools: grinders, buffers, sanders, spray cans, sockets and wrenches. Cans of glossy paint, half empty, labels lined with residual drips. The pile of blankets in the corner where the dog slept and pussy was traded for crank. Pin-ups cluttered a corner of wall, feathered hair and hairy bush. A random beauty covered a gap in the wall, bisected by a ray of light, a wet stain from the crack she covered. An aggressive look from a submissive position–something he understood too well.

The front door, sloppy cuts forced an awkward fit, an ornate replacement for a flat panel that had been kicked in. Behind the door, kitchen and living room shared a space that was divided by appliances. The TV backed to the stove. The refrigerator sat awkwardly out from the wall, fueled by an orange cord held above the doorway by nails. The kitchen window looked out onto a neighboring yard filled with American muscle cars. The sight provoked a bitter envy; some of the neighbor's cars were in operational condition. The walls of the room were more or less yellow, altered by years of smoke and grease, spackle and violence. The floors were soft wood, occasionally mopped but never sealed, stained with rot near the sink, crusted with glue and occasional chunks of linoleum. Thick mounds of dog hair lined the perimeter.

The living room was defined by the dining table, a proud, sturdy structure, with surface scratches and black bits of dried food stuck in decorative grooves. The chairs were thick-spindled Windsors, though only three remained for the family of four. A metal folding chair filled in the gap. There wasn't room for a recliner, so homemade pillows with their wavy edges and frayed tassels slumped about the floor, threadbare comfort accompanied daytime TV.

The first room down the unlit hall was the eldest child's space, a daughter. Sheet for a door. The room was a yellow box with painted yellow floors. Sunshine in pigment. A white bed frame spotted with rust, yellow flowered sheets. The box spring and bedrails were strata, layers of metal and shimmering polyester. A dainty table once held stuffed animals, then filled with perfumes, make-up, jewelry, studded leather bands and silver skulls. Dandelions and Holly Hobby gave way to metal magazine pin-ups: Lars, Vince, Axel, Tommy and Slash. Ratted hair, devil worshipers, flipping the bird with the ring finger-the wrong finger, sanitized rebellion from teenage fan magazines.

Milk crates filled with old Barbies and plastic horses, covered by clothes, sitting behind the threshold of the doorless closet. Thrift store dresses cascaded over boxes. Dirty dishes piled by the bed. Holes kicked, punched into the walls. A doll dressed in purple satin with a bulb extending from its broken head illuminated piles of wet towels and tattered jeans.

Next-door was the bathroom, orange vinyl tiles embossed with gold accents. The smells of shit and mildew, chalky white spots on a yellow shower curtain, black corners around the tub. The septic tank could no longer handle toilet paper, so a trash can was used instead. Hot water required a vice grip.

In the parent's room, a bent, dented and tarnished brass bed, unmade, piled with filthy blankets, an orgy of Navajo pattern and giant chrysanthemums. The smells: dirt, feet, sex, grease and dog. The mother's space was a lowboy piled with dusty colognes, inherited jewelry boxes, clothes, books, keepsakes, papers, sundries and a small black and white TV. The father's highboy piled with collapsing boxes of clothes that came from nowhere, that he had no intention of wearing, rock-n-roll eight tracks, songs that embarrassed his wife, the porn that she feared. Magazines dropped behind the bed, having served their instructional purpose.

The hallway terminated at the son's room, the youngest child, the end of the family line. His room began pink, with crudely varnished pine floors, Star Wars curtains, sheets, and a paper Star Trek mobile hung above his Victorian dolly. His dresser, a mahogany hand me down, painted, peeling blue. Pencils and papers strewn over the floor. He couldn't get paint, so he worked with water smearing the lines of markers. Books, piled: Shakespeare on top, Joe Orton, Jean Genet, witchcraft tucked underneath, spines facing the wall. The room ended up blue with a clumsy white horizontal stripe, oddly placed posters covering holes. Door splashed with car paint, song lyrics brushed in place with Whiteout, words for feelings he wanted to understand enough to forget.

With the exception of crank labs that explode vertically, blowing a charred hole through layers of sagging shingle and leaving the exterior walls unscathed, it was difficult to tell which houses had been abandoned. There was a pervasive aesthetic of disrepair or disassemble. A missing door didn't mean empty, just broken. Broken down, broken in, a peeling veneer revealing the skeleton of a hollow core. Several families might live behind thin walls, protected only by an aluminum mesh over the entrance. Their pooled resources fed habits and naked children, covered a miniscule mortgage taken against the home, that meager inheritance. Dreams and speed don't come cheap.

Discerning decrepit from abandoned is a matter of connoisseurship. After people leave, the walls are the first to go. Kids don't start the destruction; they finish it. Kids don't understand that a house is a copper mine, and the junk of its guts gets traded for cash.

After pans and clothes are packed into the bed of an El Camino, under flashlight and moonlight, the house is open to all. The neighbors' friendly waving hands become the desperado's violent grasp: punching through plaster, pulling out wire. Wad it up, burn it up. The plastic housing melts away leaving pure salvage value in its place. Maybe 80 cents a pound.

Toilets, swag lamps, faucets and drawer pulls are currency, replacements for something broken, saved for a special occasion. Poverty is navigated with a stockpile of porcelain and pull-chains. Potential use, potential value, trash to trade in a time of need.

When kids come, windows break. It's an introduction to transgression, breaking a familial structure from a safe distance. The duration of a rock's flight through space allows plausible deniability, the warped reflection of total destruction.

Graffiti inscribes new values: loves and hates, cunts and fucks, lyrics for feelings, gypsum dust scraped into lines.

Bodies replace Barbies. Square haircuts and ink pen makeovers become the taste of tongue and sweat, the smells of crotch and jerky breath. Coke cans become beer cans, black label bottles among cigarette butts. Practicing addiction is a private affair; its public premier must be convincing. Growing up means learning tolerance, but still, no niggers allowed.

Front yards were junkyards and back yards were worse. The front yard held forgotten fruit trees, planted for sustenance by a depression era mother. Most remained small, withered. Only one was suitable for climbing. Debris piled around trees, the strewn remains of home improvement. A rusty lawnmower, poised to tackle the weeds that grew up through its wheels. A useless red wagon, leaning at one corner, its red body rinsed with rust. The metal became a jagged filigree mapping an assortment of lost continents. Traffic and neglect had yellowed the path to a patch of lawn covered with misshapen swatches of found carpet, quilted dirt for children to play on. It wasn't the useful rectangle of organized sport, but the shape of cancer and the color of cartoons, encroached by filth, hemmed in by a ditch. On the porch, dozens of plants in crumbling terra cotta. Potted landscape surrounded the ass end of a leaky swamp cooler protruding from a window. Kitten's Ear, Spider Plant, Martians' Toes, browning from neglect, but still a mother's finest passion.

In a dusty side yard sat a Chevy Citation, red where it wasn't primer grey, a white hood and no wheels. It wasn't preserved on jacks, so it sank to the fenders, slowly claimed by winters' mud. A convertible Fiat missing its top, sat under a cover that sagged into the cab, full of rain, dirt and rotting leaves.

On the porch, boxes of miscellanea, clothes and screws, Greasy rubber seals and romance novels, knick-knacks and porno mags all mingled in molding cardboard. Fruits fell from the large tree, the one that survived against total neglect. Mulberries smashed into the driveway, smeared under the tread of late night visitors. A grotesque brown film covered the cement and an alcoholic smell invaded the house. Cars slid to a stop over the mess of pulp and seed. But nobody ever tried to clean it up; winter rains washed the mess away.

The back yard was divided by a ramshackle building, an adult-sized hideout, built over the remains of a garden. Three cars lined the flaccid fence from the gate to the sagging sliding garage door. Cars were parked to resemble order: an Impala whose front end was a smashed black cavity without an engine, a Corvair missing a transmission, a pile of pieces, Camaro and/or Bel Aire. Dream cars in nightmare condition, collected for restoration, a quick buck off an allegedly meager task. Poor investment machinery. They rested under the canopy of pecan trees, among leaves piled thick, stifling the weeds that weren't already stunted by the seepage of oil and battery acid.

Behind the shop, garage, adult playroom or fire hazard, was a large unused space of yard. Raspberries were once grown there, harvested and sold at the local market. But the bushes were burnt, and that part of the yard was left fallow. Overgrown, green became yellow during summer droughts. A lone vine survived the scorch. At the farthest end was a pile of rubble, walls of broken concrete arranged in a circle holding a heaping mound of garbage.

The backyard was off limits. The patriarch built his skull and bones, his degenerate clubhouse, a grown-up fort made with scraps culled from construction site dumpsters. Blue tarp roof, no windows, total privacy, secrecy within the patchwork of plywood. Stained, dusty wooden crates lined the walls, filled with the clunky greasy parts of cars, a prodigious collection of screws, nuts and bolts, a rolling metal chest of tools: grinders, buffers, sanders, spray cans, sockets and wrenches. Cans of glossy paint, half empty, labels lined with residual drips. The pile of blankets in the corner where the dog slept and pussy was traded for crank. Pin-ups cluttered a corner of wall, feathered hair and hairy bush. A random beauty covered a gap in the wall, bisected by a ray of light, a wet stain from the crack she covered. An aggressive look from a submissive position–something he understood too well.

The front door, sloppy cuts forced an awkward fit, an ornate replacement for a flat panel that had been kicked in. Behind the door, kitchen and living room shared a space that was divided by appliances. The TV backed to the stove. The refrigerator sat awkwardly out from the wall, fueled by an orange c he kitchen window looked out onto a neighboring yard filled with American muscle cars. The sight provoked a bitter envy; some of the neighbor's cars were in operational condition. The walls of the room were more or less yellow, altered by years of smoke and grease, spackle and violence. The floors were soft wood, occasionally mopped but never sealed, stained with rot near the sink, crusted with glue and occasional chunks of linoleum. Thick mounds of dog hair lined the perimeter.

The living room was defined by the dining table, a proud, sturdy structure, with surface scratches and black bits of dried food stuck in decorative grooves. The chairs were thick-spindled Windsors, though only three remained for the family of four. A metal folding chair filled in the gap. There wasn't room for a recliner, so homemade pillows with their wavy edges and frayed tassels slumped about the floor, threadbare comfort accompanied daytime TV.

The first room down the unlit hall was the eldest child's space, a daughter. Sheet for a door. The room was a yellow box with painted yellow floors. Sunshine in pigment. A white bed frame spotted with rust, yellow flowered sheets. The box spring and bedrails were strata, layers of metal and shimmering polyester. A dainty table once held stuffed animals, then filled with perfumes, make-up, jewelry, studded leather bands and silver skulls. Dandelions and Holly Hobby gave way to metal magazine pin-ups: Lars, Vince, Axel, Tommy and Slash. Ratted hair, devil worshipers, flipping the bird with the ring finger-the wrong finger, sanitized rebellion from teenage fan magazines.

Milk crates filled with old Barbies and plastic horses, covered by clothes, sitting behind the threshold of the doorless closet. Thrift store dresses cascaded over boxes. Dirty dishes piled by the bed. Holes kicked, punched into the walls. A doll dressed in purple satin with a bulb extending from its broken head illuminated piles of wet towels and tattered jeans.

Next-door was the bathroom, orange vinyl tiles embossed with gold accents. The smells of shit and mildew, chalky white spots on a yellow shower curtain, black corners around the tub. The septic tank could no longer handle toilet paper, so a trash can was used instead. Hot water required a vice grip.

In the parent's room, a bent, dented and tarnished brass bed, unmade, piled with filthy blankets, an orgy of Navajo pattern and giant chrysanthemums. The smells: dirt, feet, sex, grease and dog. The mother's space was a lowboy piled with dusty colognes, inherited jewelry boxes, clothes, books, keepsakes, papers, sundries and a small black and white TV. The father's highboy piled with collapsing boxes of clothes that came from nowhere, that he had no intention of wearing, rock-n-roll eight tracks, songs that embarrassed his wife, the porn that she feared. Magazines dropped behind the bed, having served their instructional purpose.

The hallway terminated at the son's room, the youngest child, the end of the family line. His room began pink, with crudely varnished pine floors, Star Wars curtains, sheets, and a paper Star Trek mobile hung above his Victorian dolly. His dresser, a mahogany hand me down, painted, peeling blue. Pencils and papers strewn over the floor. He couldn't get paint, so he worked with water smearing the lines of markers. Books, piled: Shakespeare on top, Joe Orton, Jean Genet, witchcraft tucked underneath, spines facing the wall. The room ended up blue with a clumsy white horizontal stripe, oddly placed posters covering holes. Door splashed with car paint, song lyrics brushed in place with Whiteout, words for feelings he wanted to understand enough to forget.

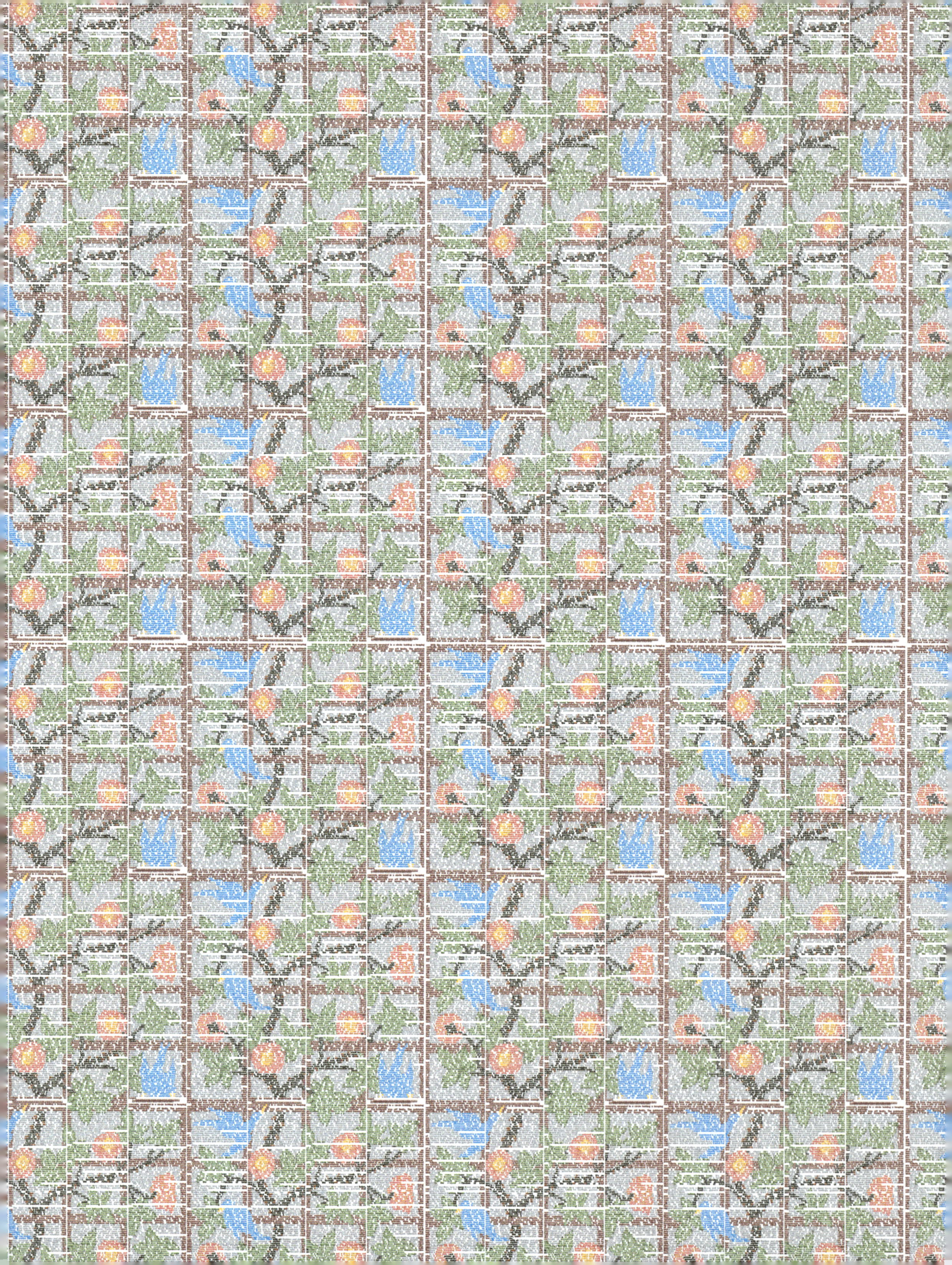

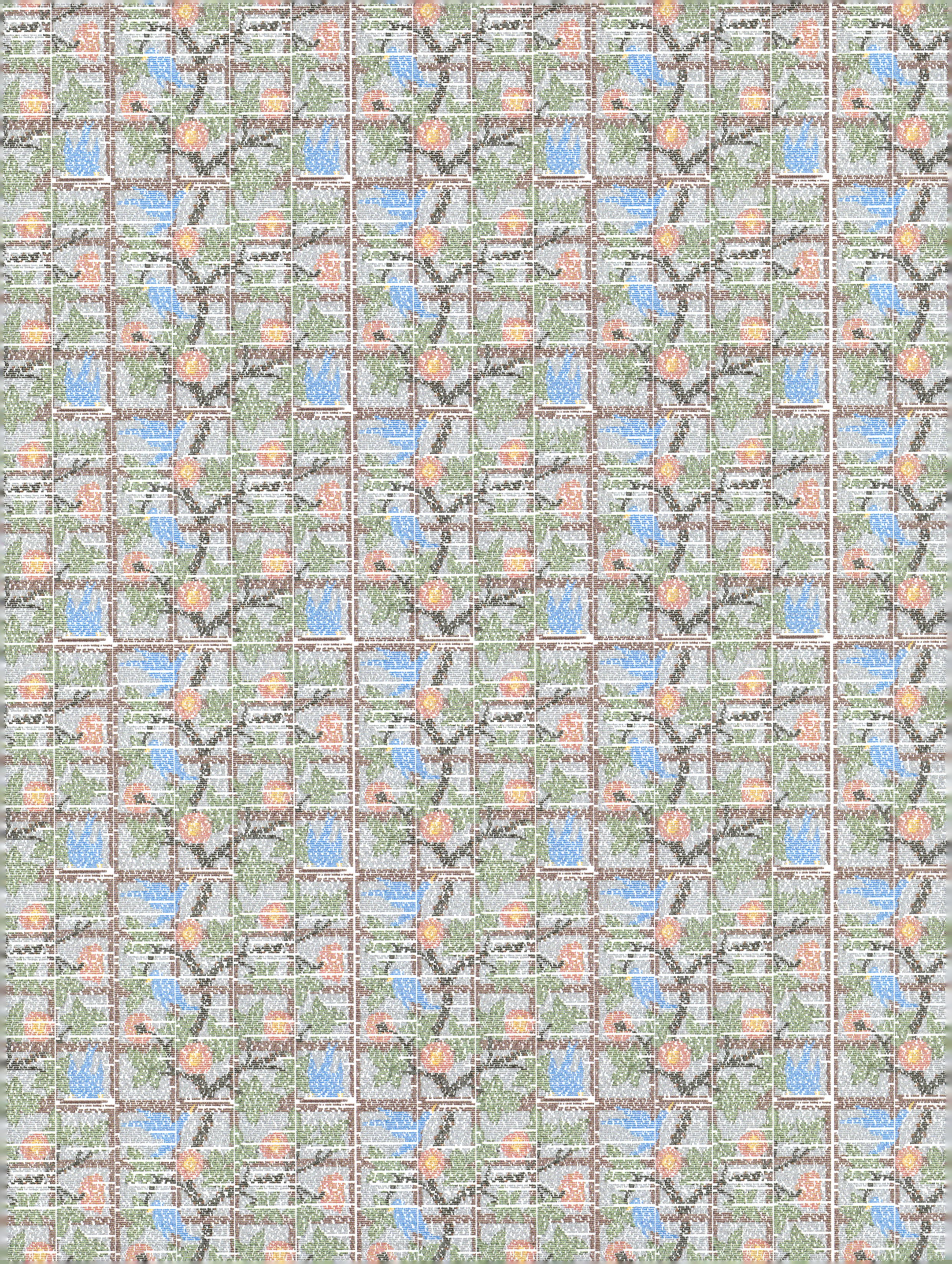

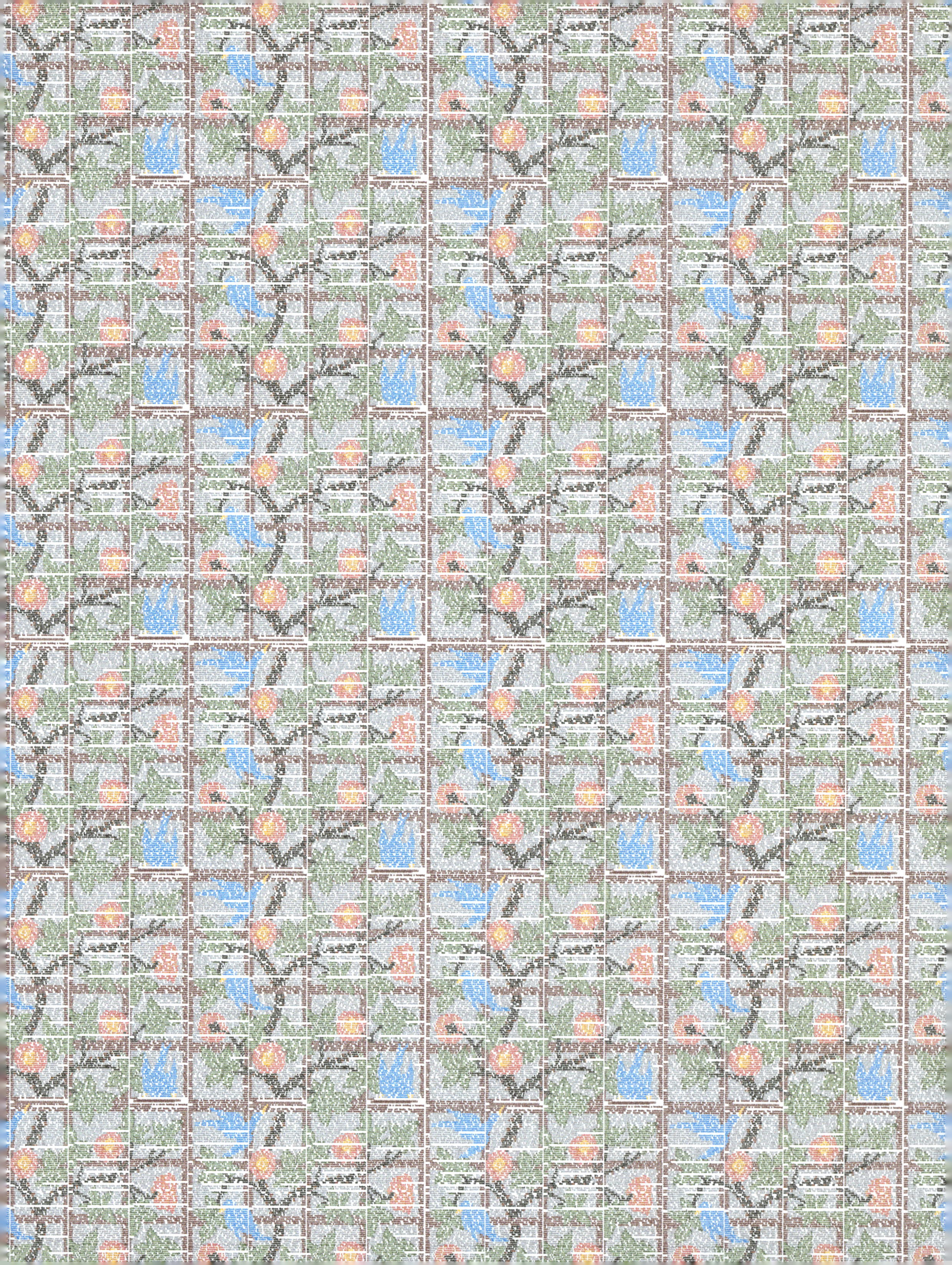

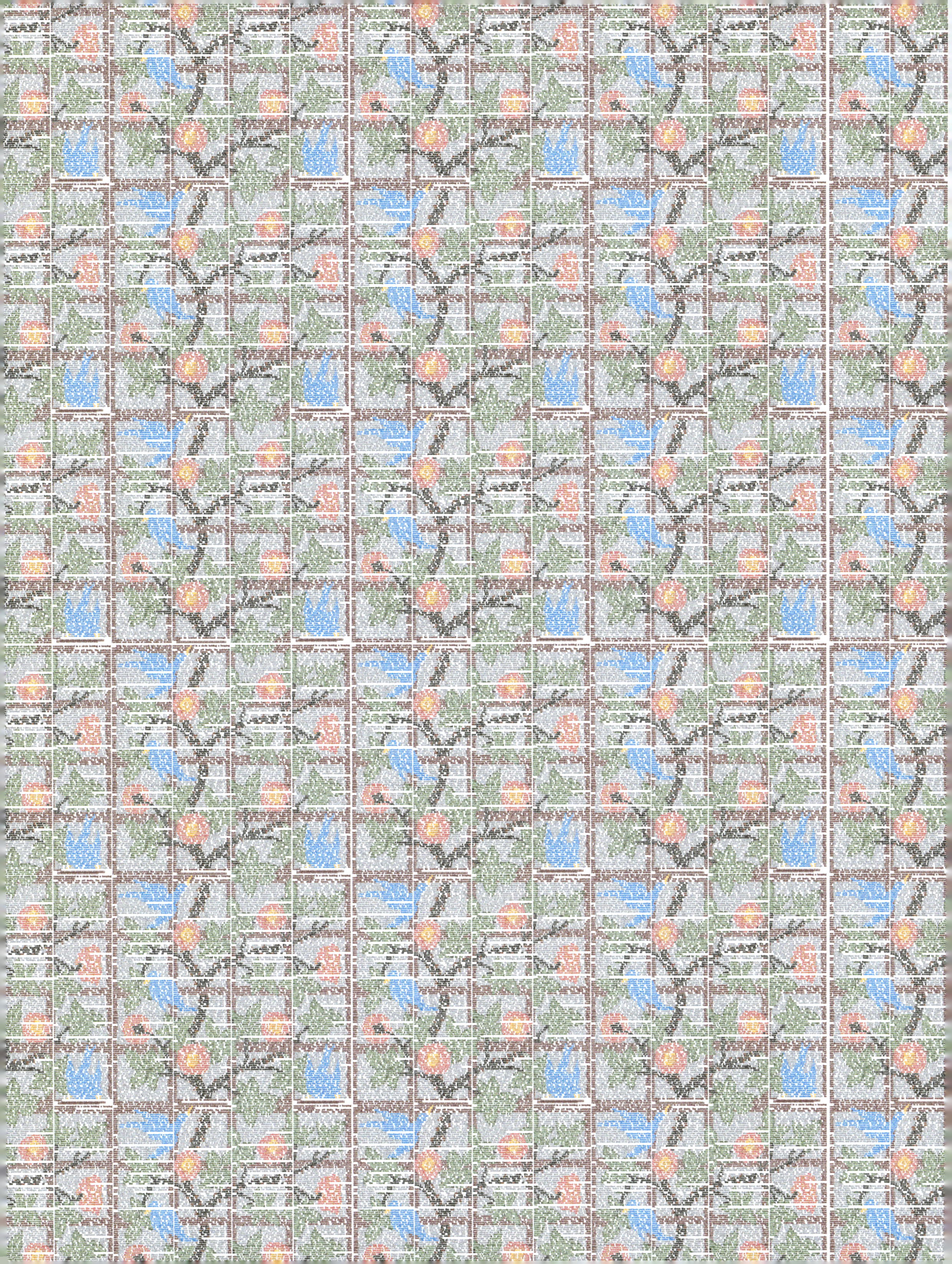

With the exception of crank labs that explode vertically, blowing a charred hole through layers of sagging shingle and leaving the exterior walls unscathed, it was difficult to tell which houses had been abandoned. There was a pervasive aesthetic of disrepair or disassemble. A missing door didn't mean empty, just broken. Broken down, broken in, a peeling veneer revealing the skeleton of a hollow core. Several families might live behind thin walls, protected only by an aluminum mesh over the entrance. Their pooled resources fed habits and naked children, covered a miniscule mortgage taken against the home, that meager inheritance. Dreams and speed don't come cheap.

Discerning decrepit from abandoned is a matter of connoisseurship. After people leave, the walls are the first to go. Kids don't start the destruction; they finish it. Kids don't understand that a house is a copper mine, and the junk of its guts gets traded for cash.

After pans and clothes are packed into the bed of an El Camino, under flashlight and moonlight, the house is open to all. The neighbors' friendly waving hands become the desperado's violent grasp: punching through plaster, pulling out wire. Wad it up, burn it up. The plastic housing melts away leaving pure salvage value in its place. Maybe 80 cents a pound.

Toilets, swag lamps, faucets and drawer pulls are currency, replacements for something broken, saved for a special occasion. Poverty is navigated with a stockpile of porcelain and pull-chains. Potential use, potential value, trash to trade in a time of need.

When kids come, windows break. It's an introduction to transgression, breaking a familial structure from a safe distance. The duration of a rock's flight through space allows plausible deniability, the warped reflection of total destruction.

Graffiti inscribes new values: loves and hates, cunts and fucks, lyrics for feelings, gypsum dust scraped into lines.

Bodies replace Barbies. Square haircuts and ink pen makeovers become the taste of tongue and sweat, the smells of crotch and jerky breath. Coke cans become beer cans, black label bottles among cigarette butts. Practicing addiction is a private affair; its public premier must be convincing. Growing up means learning tolerance, but still, no niggers allowed.

Front yards were junkyards and back yards were worse. The front yard held forgotten fruit trees, planted for sustenance by a depression era mother. Most remained small, withered. Only one was suitable for climbing. Debris piled around trees, the strewn remains of home improvement. A rusty lawnmower, poised to tackle the weeds that grew up through its wheels. A useless red wagon, leaning at one corner, its red body rinsed with rust. The metal became a jagged filigree mapping an assortment of lost continents. Traffic and neglect had yellowed the path to a patch of lawn covered with misshapen swatches of found carpet, quilted dirt for children to play on. It wasn't the useful rectangle of organized sport, but the shape of cancer and the color of cartoons, encroached by filth, hemmed in by a ditch. On the porch, dozens of plants in crumbling terra cotta. Potted landscape surrounded the ass end of a leaky swamp cooler protruding from a window. Kitten's Ear, Spider Plant, Martians' Toes, browning from neglect, but still a mother's finest passion.

In a dusty side yard sat a Chevy Citation, red where it wasn't primer grey, a white hood and no wheels. It wasn't preserved on jacks, so it sank to the fenders, slowly claimed by winters' mud. A convertible Fiat missing its top, sat under a cover that sagged into the cab, full of rain, dirt and rotting leaves.

On the porch, boxes of miscellanea, clothes and screws, Greasy rubber seals and romance novels, knick-knacks and porno mags all mingled in molding cardboard. Fruits fell from the large tree, the one that survived against total neglect. Mulberries smashed into the driveway, smeared under the tread of late night visitors. A grotesque brown film covered the cement and an alcoholic smell invaded the house. Cars slid to a stop over the mess of pulp and seed. But nobody ever tried to clean it up; winter rains washed the mess away.

The back yard was divided by a ramshackle building, an adult-sized hideout, built over the remains of a garden. Three cars lined the flaccid fence from the gate to the sagging sliding garage door. Cars were parked to resemble order: an Impala whose front end was a smashed black cavity without an engine, a Corvair missing a transmission, a pile of pieces, Camaro and/or Bel Aire. Dream cars in nightmare condition, collected for restoration, a quick buck off an allegedly meager task. Poor investment machinery. They rested under the canopy of pecan trees, among leaves piled thick, stifling the weeds that weren't already stunted by the seepage of oil and battery acid.

Behind the shop, garage, adult playroom or fire hazard, was a large unused space of yard. Raspberries were once grown there, harvested and sold at the local market. But the bushes were burnt, and that part of the yard was left fallow. Overgrown, green became yellow during summer droughts. A lone vine survived the scorch. At the farthest end was a pile of rubble, walls of broken concrete arranged in a circle holding a heaping mound of garbage.

The backyard was off limits. The patriarch built his skull and bones, his degenerate clubhouse, a grown-up fort made with scraps culled from construction site dumpsters. Blue tarp roof, no windows, total privacy, secrecy within the patchwork of plywood. Stained, dusty wooden crates lined the walls, filled with the clunky greasy parts of cars, a prodigious collection of screws, nuts and bolts, a rolling metal chest of tools: grinders, buffers, sanders, spray cans, sockets and wrenches. Cans of glossy paint, half empty, labels lined with residual drips. The pile of blankets in the corner where the dog slept and pussy was traded for crank. Pin-ups cluttered a corner of wall, feathered hair and hairy bush. A random beauty covered a gap in the wall, bisected by a ray of light, a wet stain from the crack she covered. An aggressive look from a submissive position–something he understood too well.

The front door, sloppy cuts forced an awkward fit, an ornate replacement for a flat panel that had been kicked in. Behind the door, kitchen and living room shared a space that was divided by appliances. The TV backed to the stove. The refrigerator sat awkwardly out from the wall, fueled by an orange cord held above the doorway by nails. The kitchen window looked out onto a neighboring yard filled with American muscle cars. The sight provoked a bitter envy; some of the neighbor's cars were in operational condition. The walls of the room were more or less yellow, altered by years of smoke and grease, spackle and violence. The floors were soft wood, occasionally mopped but never sealed, stained with rot near the sink, crusted with glue and occasional chunks of linoleum. Thick mounds of dog hair lined the perimeter.

The living room was defined by the dining table, a proud, sturdy structure, with surface scratches and black bits of dried food stuck in decorative grooves. The chairs were thick-spindled Windsors, though only three remained for the family of four. A metal folding chair filled in the gap. There wasn't room for a recliner, so homemade pillows with their wavy edges and frayed tassels slumped about the floor, threadbare comfort accompanied daytime TV.

The first room down the unlit hall was the eldest child's space, a daughter. Sheet for a door. The room was a yellow box with painted yellow floors. Sunshine in pigment. A white bed frame spotted with rust, yellow flowered sheets. The box spring and bedrails were strata, layers of metal and shimmering polyester. A dainty table once held stuffed animals, then filled with perfumes, make-up, jewelry, studded leather bands and silver skulls. Dandelions and Holly Hobby gave way to metal magazine pin-ups: Lars, Vince, Axel, Tommy and Slash. Ratted hair, devil worshipers, flipping the bird with the ring finger-the wrong finger, sanitized rebellion from teenage fan magazines.

Milk crates filled with old Barbies and plastic horses, covered by clothes, sitting behind the threshold of the doorless closet. Thrift store dresses cascaded over boxes. Dirty dishes piled by the bed. Holes kicked, punched into the walls. A doll dressed in purple satin with a bulb extending from its broken head illuminated piles of wet towels and tattered jeans.

Next-door was the bathroom, orange vinyl tiles embossed with gold accents. The smells of shit and mildew, chalky white spots on a yellow shower curtain, black corners around the tub. The septic tank could no longer handle toilet paper, so a trash can was used instead. Hot water required a vice grip.

In the parent's room, a bent, dented and tarnished brass bed, unmade, piled with filthy blankets, an orgy of Navajo pattern and giant chrysanthemums. The smells: dirt, feet, sex, grease and dog. The mother's space was a lowboy piled with dusty colognes, inherited jewelry boxes, clothes, books, keepsakes, papers, sundries and a small black and white TV. The father's highboy piled with collapsing boxes of clothes that came from nowhere, that he had no intention of wearing, rock-n-roll eight tracks, songs that embarrassed his wife, the porn that she feared. Magazines dropped behind the bed, having served their instructional purpose.

The hallway terminated at the son's room, the youngest child, the end of the family line. His room began pink, with crudely varnished pine floors, Star Wars curtains, sheets, and a paper Star Trek mobile hung above his Victorian dolly. His dresser, a mahogany hand me down, painted, peeling blue. Pencils and papers strewn over the floor. He couldn't get paint, so he worked with water smearing the lines of markers. Books, piled: Shakespeare on top, Joe Orton, Jean Genet, witchcraft tucked underneath, spines facing the wall. The room ended up blue with a clumsy white horizontal stripe, oddly placed posters covering holes. Door splashed with car paint, song lyrics brushed in place with Whiteout, words for feelings he wanted to understand enough to forget.

Bats & Poppies
after Maurice Pillard Verneuil

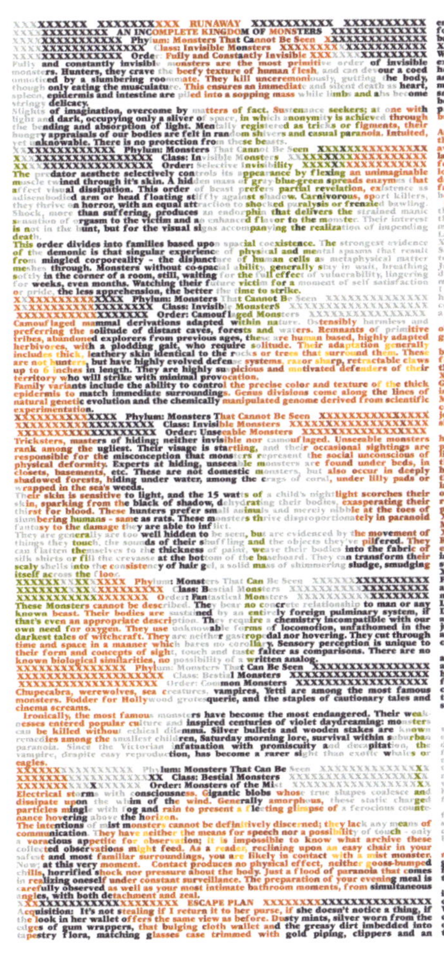

XXXXXXXXXX XXXXXXXXXXX RUNAWAY XXXXXXXXXXX XXXXXXXXXX
XXXXXXXXXXXXX AN INCOMPLETE KINGDOM OF MONSTERS XXXXXXXXXXXXXX
XXXXXXXXXXXXXXX Phylum: Monsters That Cannot Be Seen XXXXXXXXXXXXXXX
XXXXXXXXXXXXXXXXXX Class: Invisible Monsters XXXXXXXXXXXXXXXXXXXXXX
XXXXXXXXXXXXXXX Order: Fully and Constantly Invisible XXXXXXXXXXXXXXXXX

Fully and constantly invisible monsters are the most primitive order of invisible monsters. Hunters, they crave the beefy texture of human flesh, and can devour a coed unnoticed by a slumbering roommate. They kill unceremoniously, gutting the body, though only eating the musculature. This ensures an immediate and silent death as heart, spleen, epidermis and intestine are piled into a sopping mass while limbs and abs become stringy delicacy.

Slights of imagination, overcome by matters of fact. Sustenance seekers; at one with light and dark, occupying only a sliver of space, in which anonymity is achieved through the bending and absorption of light. Mentally registered as tricks or figments, their hungry appraisals of our bodies are felt in random shivers and casual paranoia. Intuited, yet unknowable. There is no protection from these beasts.

XXXXXXXXXXXXXXX Phylum: Monsters That Cannot Be Seen XXXXXXXXXXXXXXXXX
XXXXXXXXXXXXXXXXXXXXX Class: Invisible Monsters XXXXXXXXXXXXXXXXXXXX
XXXXXXXXXXXXXXXXXXXXX Order: Selective Invisibility XXXXXXXXXXXXXXXXXXX

The predator aesthete selectively controls its appearance by flexing an unimaginable muscle twined through it's skin. A hidden mass of gray blue-green spreads enzymes that affect visual dissipation. This order of beast prefers partial revelation, existence as adisembodied arm or head floating stiffly against shadow. Carnivorous, sport killers, they thrive on horror, with an equal attraction to shocked paralysis or frenzied bawling. Shock, more than suffering, produces an endorphin that delivers the strained manic sensation of orgasm to the victim and an enhanced flavor to the monster. Their interest is not in the hunt, but for the visual signs accompanying the realization of impending death.

This order divides into families based upon spacial coexistence. The strongest evidence of the demonic is that singular experience of physical and mental spasms that result from mingled corporeality - the disjuncture of human cells as metaphysical matter meshes through. Monsters without co-spacial ability, generally stay in wait, breathing softly in the corner of a room, still, waiting for the full effect of vulnerability, lingering for weeks, even months. Watching their future victim for a moment of self satisfaction or pride, the less apprehension, the better the time to strike.

XXXXXXXXXXXXXXXX Phylum: Monsters That Cannot Be Seen XXXXXXXXXXXXXXX
XXXXXXXXXXXXXXXXXXXXX Class: Invisible MonsterS XXXXXXXXXXXXXXXXXXXXX
XXXXXXXXXXXXXXXXXXXX Order: Camouflaged Monsters XXXXXXXXXXXXXXXXX

Camouflaged mammal derivations adapted within nature. Ostensibly harmless and preferring the solitude of distant caves, forests and waters. Remnants of primitive tribes, abandoned explorers from previous ages, these are human based, highly adapted herbivores, with a plodding gait, who require solitude. Their adaptation generally includes thick, leathery skin identical to the rocks or trees that surround them. These are not hunters, but have highly evolved defense systems, razor sharp, retractable claws up to 6 inches in length. They are highly suspicious and motivated defenders of their territory who will strike with minimal provocation.

Family variants include the ability to control the precise color and texture of the thick epidermis to match immediate surroundings. Genus divisions come along the lines of natural genetic evolution and the chemically manipulated genome derived from scientific experimentation.

XXXXXXXXXXXXXXX Phylum: Monsters That Cannot Be Seen XXXXXXXXXXXXXXX
XXXXXXXXXXXXXXXXXXXXX Class: Invisible Monsters XXXXXXXXXXXXXXXXXXXXX
XXXXXXXXXXXXXXXXXXXXXX Order: Unseeable Monsters XXXXXXXXXXXXXXXXXX

Tricksters, masters of hiding; neither invisible nor camouflaged. Unseeable monsters rank among the ugliest. Their visage is startling, and their occasional sightings are responsible for the misconception that monsters represent the social unconscious of physical deformity. Experts at hiding, unseeable monsters are found under beds, in closets, basements, etc. These are not domestic monsters, but also occur in deeply shadowed forests, hiding under water, among the crags of coral, under lilly pads or wrapped in the sea's weeds.

Their skin is sensitive to light, and the 15 watts of a child's nightlight scorches their skin, sparking from the black of shadow, dehydrating their bodies, exasperating their thirst for blood. These hunters prefer small animals and merely nibble at the toes of slumbering humans - same as rats. These monsters thrive disproportionately in paranoid fantasy to the damage they are able to inflict.

They are generally are too well hidden to be seen, but are evidenced by the movement of things they touch, the sounds of their shuffling and the objects they've pilfered. They can flatten themselves to the thickness of paint, weave their bodies into the fabric of silk shirts or fill the crevasse at the bottom of the baseboard. They can transform their scaly shells into the consistency of hair gel, a solid mass of shimmering sludge, smudging itself across the floor.

XXXXXXXXXXXXXXXXX Phylum: Monsters That Can Be Seen XXXXXXXXXXXXXXXXXX
XXXXXXXXXXXXXXXXXXXXXXX Class: Bestial Monsters XXXXXXXXXXXXXXXXXXXXX
XXXXXXXXXXXXXXXXXXXXXX Order: Fantastical Monsters XXXXXXXXXXXXXXXXXX

These Monsters cannot be described. They bear no concrete relationship to man or any known beast. Their bodies are sustained by an entirely foreign pulminary system, if that's even an appropriate description. They require a chemistry incompatible with our own need for oxygen. They use unknowable forms of locomotion, unfathomed in the darkest tales of witchcraft. They are neither gastropodal nor hovering. They cut through time and space in a manner which bares no corollary. Sensory perception is unique to their form and concepts of sight, touch and taste falter as comparisons. There are no known biological similarities, no possibility of a written analog.

XXXXXXXXXXXXXXXXX Phylum: Monsters That Can Be Seen XXXXXXXXXXXXXXXXXX
XXXXXXXXXXXXXXXXXXXXXXX Class: Bestial Monsters XXXXXXXXXXXXXXXXXXXXX
XXXXXXXXXXXXXXXXXXXXX Order: Common Monsters XXXXXXXXXXXXXXXXXXXXX

Chupecabra, werewolves, sea creatures, vampires, Yetti are among the most famous monsters. Fodder for Hollywood grotesquerie, and the staples of cautionary tales and cinema screams.

Ironically, the most famous monsters have become the most endangered. Their weaknesses entered popular culture and inspired centuries of violet daydreaming: monsters can be killed without ethical dilemma. Silver bullets and wooden stakes are known remedies among the smallest children, Saturday morning lore, survival within suburban paranoia. Since the Victorian infatuation with promiscuity and decapitation, the vampire, despite easy reproduction, has become a rarer sight than exotic whales or eagles.

XXXXXXXXXXXXXXXX Phylum: Monsters That Can Be Seen XXXXXXXXXXXXXXXXXX
XXXXXXXXXXXXXXXXXXXXXX Class: Bestial Monsters XXXXXXXXXXXXXXXXXXXXX
XXXXXXXXXXXXXXXX Order: Monsters of the Mist XXXXXXXXXXXXXXXXXXXXXX

Electrical storms with consciousness. Gigantic blobs whose true shapes coalesce and dissipate upon the whim of the wind. Generally amorphous, these static charged particles mingle with fog and rain to present a fleeting glimpse of a ferocious countenance hovering above the horizon.

The intentions of mist monsters cannot be definitively discerned; they lack any means of communication. They have neither the means for speech nor a possibility of touch - only a voracious appetite for observation; it is impossible to know what archive these collected observations might feed. As a reader, reclining upon an easy chair in your safest and most familiar surroundings, you are likely in contact with a mist monster. Now; at this very moment. Contact produces no physical effect, neither goose-bumped chills, horrified shock nor pressure about the body. Just a flood of paranoia that comes in realizing oneself under constant surveillance. The preparation of your evening meal is carefully observed as well as your most intimate bathroom moments, from simultaneous angles, with both detachment and zeal.

XXXXXXXXXXXXXXXXXXXXXX ESCAPE PLAN XXXXXXXXXXXXXXXXXXXXXXX

Acquisition: It's not stealing if I return it to her purse, if she doesn't notice a thing, if the look in her wallet offers the same view as before. Dusty mints, silver worn from the edges of gum wrappers, that bulging cloth wallet and the greasy dirt imbedded into tapestry flora, matching glasses case trimmed with gold piping, clippers and an emerboard scratched irregularly from tumbling among the guts of the purse, various forms of ID and business cards held as a block of worn corners by a cracking rubber band. Using her credit card isn't stealing, because nothing comes up missing.

XXXXXXXXXXXXXXXXXXXXXXXXXXXXXXXXXXXXXXXXXXXXXXXXXXXXXXXXXXXXXXXXXX

Winter Coat: Is there a trick to jackets? Are they a perfect apparatus designed to hold in exactly enough heat, and disperse any extra? Would the comfortable jacket I wore in a heated California classroom offer enough protection from the snow? Is the nylon shell and fluffy polyfill gauged with thermostatic accuracy? Is my parka a perpetual heat machine, gathering my 98.6 and holding it in place. If I huddle in a tiny hut along the snowy bank of a distant shore, will my jacket keep me warm? Can my own radiant warmth be harnessed against the effects of a Lake Eerie winter. Or should I dig a hole and live in partially buried hibernation; I don't want to waste my body heat on air contact. There's no buffer in my fight with the cold. Just me and the dirt.

Running away means looking ahead, imagining a new society, so it's the legacy of the Avant Garde. A fast forward to adulthood, dismantling the restrictions of organized play, the structures that keep youth dumb to the possibilities of their own bodies. Running away means envisioning a new symbolic order, wholesale rejection, unfixing successive layers of control, fashioning a new epistemology in which the wavering shadows of the forest canopy reveal more than a philosophical musing on Van Gough's shoes. There's no looking back to last year's bright red parka. It's explosion of primary colored stripes doesn't fit the future. I need something earthier, a clearer transition between Chinese factory workmanship and the scarred skins of animals that will eventually warm my body.

Once I've outgrown my city clothes, I'll transform time and nature into an aesthetic of the roughly hewn. Deerskin announces a new personal vision. I'll earn my place slitting the throat of a wide eyed buck, trading stares from bulging eyes, trading his survival for my own. There's no place for polyester, removable sleeves or applique on the banks of Lake Eerie.

XXXXXXXXXXXXXXXXXXXXXXXXXXXXXXXXXXXXXXXXXXXXXXXXXXXXXXXXXXXXXXXXXX

Snow Boots: I forget the smudge worn text from the label sewn to the back side of the tongue. It was once a clear indication of size. Maybe the european size remains, or Japanese. But where do I find Asian shoes, those cloth tops with hard plastic soles and a distinct place for the big toe? (It's what ninjas wear) I'll have to poke a hole in the top of my current pair of tennis shoes, drag my toes through dirt and grass to fray the fresh cut. I can get a replacement for worn out shoes, but not for intentional damage. The cut will have to appear poked through, mesh stretched beyond its breaking point. My mother will complain about the expense, but she expects rough play from her boy, and new shoes are a small price for evidence of masculinity.

It will be difficult to explain my interest in snow boots, but sometimes passion for an object is enough. The quantity of mother's complaints legitimize those occasional indulgences.

We'll go to the department store and I'll stand upon the measure with a salesman bowing before me. I'll make him position it, to feel the charge of his hand wrapping around my foot. Then he'll tickle the slider across arch to ball. I'll learn both length and width, though only one seems to matter.

XXXXXXXXXXXXXXXXXXXXXXXXXXXXXXXXXXXXXXXXXXXXXXXXXXXXXXXXXXXXXXXXXX

Guns and Knives: I don't like the immediacy of guns, the now of their action, their place in the trajectory of industrial progress, their remove from the intensity of the kill. Mechanical dehumanization, for both the gunman and the prey. It's a sculpture of coercion wielded with a false sense of power embodied in cinematic standoff, that circle jerk of anxiety: a group of men, each with a gun trained upon him, none with the guts to shoot.

In a new society, equality matters most. I'll have to take down a grizzly with my bear hands. It's fair if I hop on it's matted fur back, grab stiff bristled patches to hold my place on the ferocious ride. Against the bucking of his enormous trunk, I'll climb the bear like he climbs a tree, racing for life itself. I can muster the strength to crack its neck, so that he collapses under me, falls as a fleshy trembling lump, convulsions suppressed by his own heft. Powerful jaws become a cave of drool. And then, I'll need a knife to excavate the body, find the usable parts, the tastiest muscles, separate skin from bone. Something large, a blade that could double as a saw, hack the girth of a small tree and carve the bone of a large bear. An all purpose blade, something with a hand guard - safety against resistance. Single edged. Serrated - the thick, dense mass of a femur is not a score and snap proposition.

XXXXXXXXXXXXXXXXXXXXXXXXXXXXXXXXXXXXXXXXXXXXXXXXXXXXXXXXXXXXXXXXXX

Matches: Rubbing sticks together is tiring and doesn't always work.

XXXXXXXXXXXXXXXXXXXXXXXXXXXXXXXXXXXXXXXXXXXXXXXXXXXXXXXXXXXXXXXXXX

Rope: A supine lasso to snare a hare. Booby traps: a construction capable of releasing an enormous rolling boulder, or sending the sharpened stumps of trees skewering an interloping body. My new society will realize the spirit of hollywood myth, infiltrated in the stagnate cycling of suburban fantasy.

XXXXXXXXXXXXXXXXXXXXXXXXXXXXXXXXXXXXXXXXXXXXXXXXXXXXXXXXXXXXXXXXXX

Plane or Bus Ticket: In running away, how important is speed? Is the circuitous route of a bus line an adequate foil? Disperate sightings couldn't betray my ultimate goal. I would navigate up through the fields and falls of Boise, then down to the deserted planes of Lubbock. Tracing north over the ghosts of Oklahoma to the rocky landscape of the Dakota's. I'll lose myself among Chicago smoke and brick before crossing the flatlands and steel plants of Indiana. I'll have time to tour towns listed in the return addresses of junk mail: Terre Haute, Fort Wayne. The northern cities of Ohio would present a predictable path, so I'll backtrack along the Mississippi, like Huck Finn then maneuver Appalachia, making my final push north through West Virginia.

On a plane, I might travel thousands of miles in a day, only to have police waiting for my arrival at the end of registered travel. I'd make it to the frontier only to be captured like a dog, shipped back in a plastic and wire crate. I had that familiar pain of hesitation in my gut before I even reached the corner. Another practice run, testing how far I could get before anxiety took control. My fear of the world, that wide blue horizon, competing versions of American accents, and unfamiliar labels on soda pop cans. The totality of the unknown was an empty slate of transitory morals, but without the meager safety net of scheduled meals provided at the family home.

It just wasn't time to leave.

I walked in the deep ditch, looking for coke bottles, jumping up to cross the points where gravel and culvert pipe allowed automotive access. I kept a lookout for the sparkle of glass; each bottle puts another dime toward my operation. It was only three doors down, the tiny yellow house that seemed more empty than derelict. Its pieces were intact; faded wood doors, charcoal roof and sliding windows with torn and frayed, corroded metal screens, but it had an aura of abandonment. The only sign of life was a mongrel tied to a tree by a scruffy line of chain and nylon rope. He was a muscular mutt with a black monochrome of zebra stripes across his trunk, short, thick drooling muzzle and floppy velvet ears. He barked vigorously as I passed, though it wasn't personal, I might as well have been a noise on the wind. The neglected animal only raged against circumstance, the futility of an inner life, the desire for an impossible violence.

I felt envy, stepped closer to see the inflamed pink receding into nostrils and bloating from around swollen eyes. His ears tucked back, and his thick jowls revealed black spotted gums. As if by static charge, patches of wiry hair rose upon his back, while his tail curled between his legs, wound tight to the undercarriage. pressed hard against his own balls.

I tucked my fingers against my palm and offered a sniff of my hand, hoping he'd recognize our common bond and that we would find mutual serenity in the kindness of my gesture. But the growl intensified; the chain strained a deep line of pressure around the front of his neck. He pulled himself onto hind legs and kicked furiously against the dirt, trying desperately to maintain his new height, to challenge me on bipedal terms.

I moved my hand toward his nose, maintaining an inch of distance. The dog's fury increased as I drew closer. He circled with a snarl, and ended the retreat in a lunge that caught the chain in mid air, jerking the mongrel into a sideways slide across his dirty rut. We were each lost in our own fantasies of wide horizons, American accents and soda pop cans. I needed this dog, this mutt, mongrel, to know our similarities, the shared totality of our latent violence. I offered him the tip of my finger, knowing he would understand the salty metallic taste on his tiny front teeth.

XXXXXXXXXXXXXXXXXXXX Reasons to Leave XXXXXXXXXXXXXXXXXXXXXXX

Something about the possibility of air, the challenge wind makes to a tree. The losing proposition of rattling branches and a disembodied moan.þ Hickory trees are the dream of the east, something deciduous, foreign, but with a familiar phonic resemblance to "Ichabod." HIK·OR·E. IK·A·BOD. It's a world of winter terror in which trees stripped bare slash the sky. The sun is the only remaining trace of life, that light at the end of the tunnel. The great gray of its bark, the violent monochrome of night, its emptiness both proof and texture of the demonic. A moonlit, paranoid fury - still, silent and glaring. The aural similarity to a character in an outdated horror story is enough to inspire damage. This is why I chose Lake Eerie. The name alone makes the town a primary site of adolescent male freedom fantasy. Running into the forest, raging over the rustle of leaves, unfazed by the snap and cut of passing branches. Eerie is named for its preponderance of Indian cemeteries, sites of satanic ritual, for the parts of the forest that defy physics and the howling that cuts the crisp stillness of Spring. Eerie doesn't exist on any mortal coil, it's a dot on a map dotted by factories, a Motel 6, cabin and boat rentals with botched signage, fishing shacks and cozy diners. But there is an existential overlay, a space only seen by aspiring adventurers during grade school geography lessons. It's a name that captures the imagination and holds it hostage to the darkest wonderment of terrified youth.

XXXXXXXXXXXXX XXXXXX Drifter AestheticS XXXXXXXXXXXXXXXXXXX

Hitching an oblique course on the charm of my smile and the innocence of my eyes. I'm the aesthete, scanning the roadway for signs of…

The wrinkled pucker of a toothless mouth stares out from the cab of a dilapidated pick-up on a highway through the Ozarks. Armadillo tails never seem to rot. Hills as green as postcards of Ireland. A flowing scrap of a plastic sheet, hooked on bramble, glanced in passing under the distant light of a streetlamp becomes St Christopher. That hunched traveler, supported by a staff, shrouded in muslin. The distinct lines of farmland growing plants I can't identify. I overheard, "There were all these pedals and a keyhole." Sticks of shrubbery, browned grasses, lesions of red clay. The dismembered head of a sparrow. Once glassy eyes, now errant scabs in the soft order of plumage. Past the rugged remains of a neckline, rigid strings dried around a brown chunk of spine. The furry, skeletal remains of a chipmunk wearing a glass suit papered by the metallic gold of a Miller label - still attached to a curved shard of an erstwhile bottle. The yellowed ring of a condom, cracking nearby. A red 1980's Chevy Citation with a white hood. Pink bondo fender, grey primer door. Muddy lace panties. A stiffened brown bundle among dried yellow weeds, surrounded by foxtails and rabbit shit. Plastic bags caught in trees during a recent windstorm. Grocery store flags, empty, waving futilely, knowing they've already carried their weight. The ruins of roadside amusements. Splintered grey plywood, faded and peeling paint, rusted remains of mechanical supports, every bit as exotic as pyramids or Parthenon. A cardboard box labeled labeled with thick black marker: ApoCALyPse.

XXXXXXXXXXXXXXXXXXXXXXXXXX Utopia XXXXXXXXXXXXXXXXXXXXXXXXXXX

The end of the world is a purely visual event; it's intellectual legacy, the redefinition of significant form. Every smear, crack, puddle, clod, chip or shard is part of the same monochrome of existence, each just as charged as any other. Grayness fused to insignificance, rubble is the greatest technological possibility. The coveted landscape of Abercrombie abs, sublime awe smoothed into deep cuts by the force of nature, harnessed on an Ab Rocket. But rigor mortis makes that taught musculature uncomfortably bumpy, harsh, less washboard and more cheese grater. The radiant warmth of suntanned perfection converts to the fractured pattern of a dried lake bed, flaking into jagged polygons. Sexy chaos among the the fissured sheen of glass.

Desire becomes complete in the strip-down experience of aesthetic collapse. Wants are dislodged from expectation, squarely fused to texture and hue. The last man on earth isn't preserving conventions, choosing social bodies. Rather, he's an aesthete immersed in pleasant sensations, hunting for softness among the rubble.

The missing limbs of a beautiful stranger reveal personal agency as pathetic excess, a smudge of an erstwhile life. The final act of the most alluring post apocalyptic biceps was to pull the weight of his lacerated body through its own blood. Smearing; the final creative act, some ultimate expressionist gesture of streaks and pools. As his open wounds slid against the floor, he focused on the future through shrieking sobs. Velour print upholstery was never the best idea. Nearing death, he never considered his own insignificance against meteoric shrapnel, flesh eating plague, nuclear radiation or terrorist what-have-you.

Tastefully draped and perfectly soaked. Jeans, exquisitely bleached and frayed in a third world sweatshop to signify waspish rapacity, now cover a mess of separating sores too coagulated to comfortably slide ones body against.

Sweetness becomes the primary concern in a post apocalyptic necrology. Sky blue desiccated eyes, hollow in their longing, loose in their sockets, but good enough for a hard-on. He's beautiful until his skin turns that particular shade of corpse black and his belly opens up to lesions and larvae, white worms muddling through a mass of pinkish fat. His ass is a different kind of breeding ground, no longer the worst smelling part of his body. And when I kiss his mouth I hear him speak through me, like reading words in a dream, their idea comes across through mystical anonymity. The secrets his body reveals can only be translated through the random banging of typewriter keys.

Perfect bodies can't be preserved. I'd never pick a pocket to find an ID and determine some actual name. I like "Timmy," Lassie's companion in innocent kindness. "Timmy" is comfortable with the nonverbal; he understands Lassie's subjective combination of scratching and tugging, canid reports that youthful indiscretions lead a pair of small children down an abandoned well. And in the deep alone of that great black pit, they might submit to temptations equally dark. I feel love for the first time, ascribing sweetness to the dusty awkwardness of "Timmy's" broken body. It's an intense feeling, something I never knew alive, but read all through his decay. There's no illusion of forever; "Timmy" is closer to dust than reciprocity.

Love handles have the stiff malleability of clay, preserving the shape of my grip along loosely defined hips. Blood clots about the eyes and nostrils are imperfections that can be overlooked. Damage from the scruff of my own face is another story. Kissing can't become biting and chin-stubble could scratch its way down to something disturbing. Kissing through a plastic bag, hole torn to accommodate my tongue. There's no suffocation hazard, but no intimacy either. He functions at my whim, and that's the entirety of attraction. "Timmy" never complains; he understands the impending abandonment. He knows that despite everything we've shared, I have to walk away without him. My back won't sustain his weight and his limbs wouldn't withstand the strain.

It can't be rape without protest so it's making love: physical, pure, actual. "Timmy's" last moments as solid mass are devoted to me. His compound fractures approximate recent changes in architectural style; trendy to death. When the sexiest bodies resemble an accidental cave within the rubble of a collapsed building, is it wrong to want to be inside? Vultures prefer the soft hairs at the base of the belly, while insects enjoy the challenge of manilla. Electricity is gone, so refrigeration is no savior. Sunlight and soldier flies are the great enemies of lasting happiness.

I don't know how I ended up as the last one, how I survived the plague, choking dust, lack of sunlight, watermarks, rot of flood, glowing radiation or lab-created virus. I am the last man on earth; biological success. Fucking the miscellaneous remains of random bodies should be beneath me. If I'm the chosen one, why is this my choice?

If I dropped a mess of an aesthetic masterpiece from the strapped seat of an overturned Honda, dragged his randomized lump over shattered sheets of safety glass, gouging bloodless wounds across his back, would it be a rescue? Would I be entitled to exact a price on the remains of that body, indulge myself as the justified payment for my assistance, or has the forfeiture of his life made him public domain, property for the taking, something to claim with the planting of a flag. An apocalyptic Misery, though Kathy Bates was wrong, and I'm alright. Remember, my captives make no protest. He's mine, fair and square. All that's left of humanity is what's left in my head. Finders keepers. Possession is nine tenths of what's left of the law. A landscape of raw exploits and morality fabricated on the fly, It's a new society that will last until it rots.

XXXXXXXXXXXXXXXXXXXXXXX THE END XXXXXXXXXXXXXXXXXXXXXXXXXX

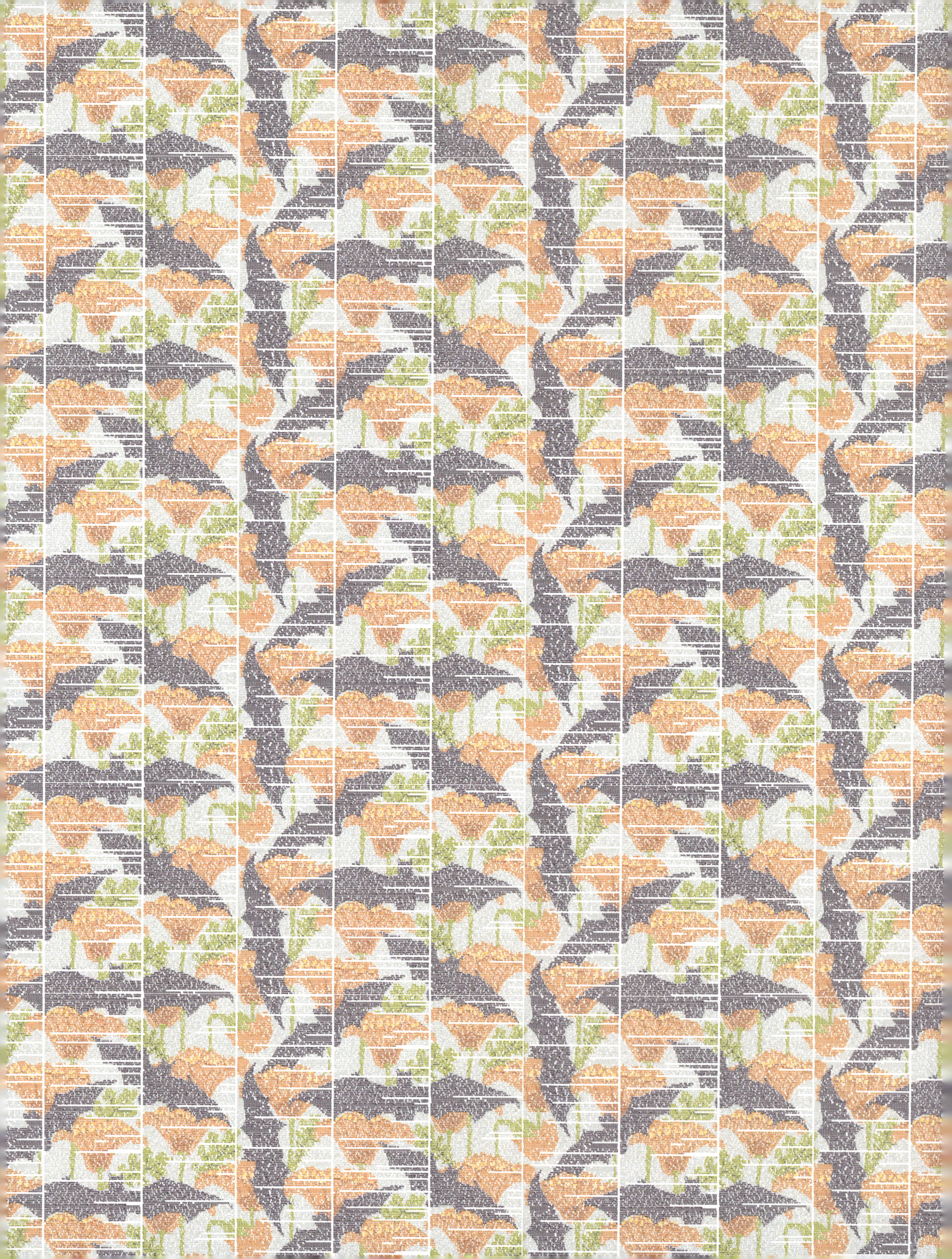

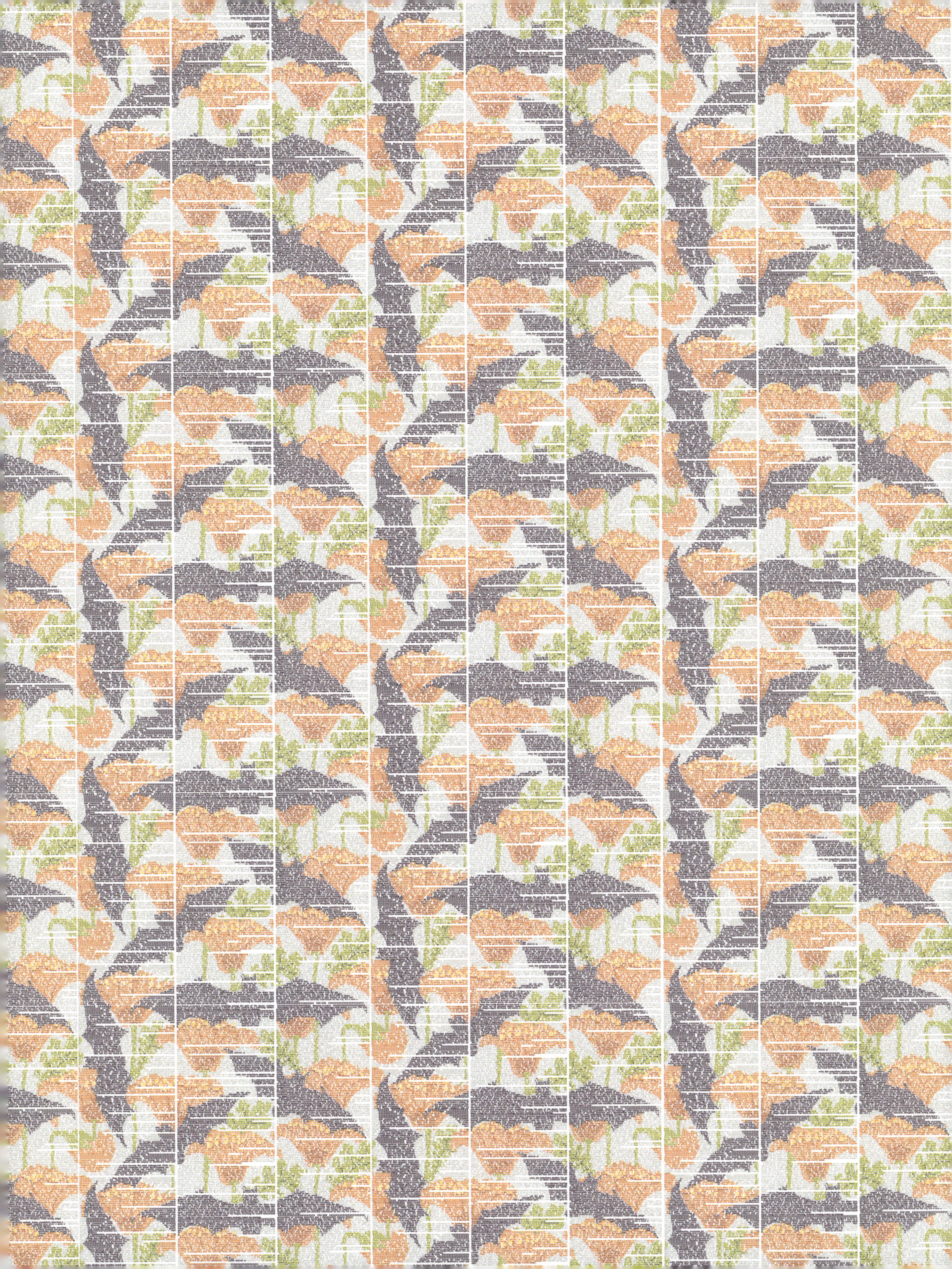

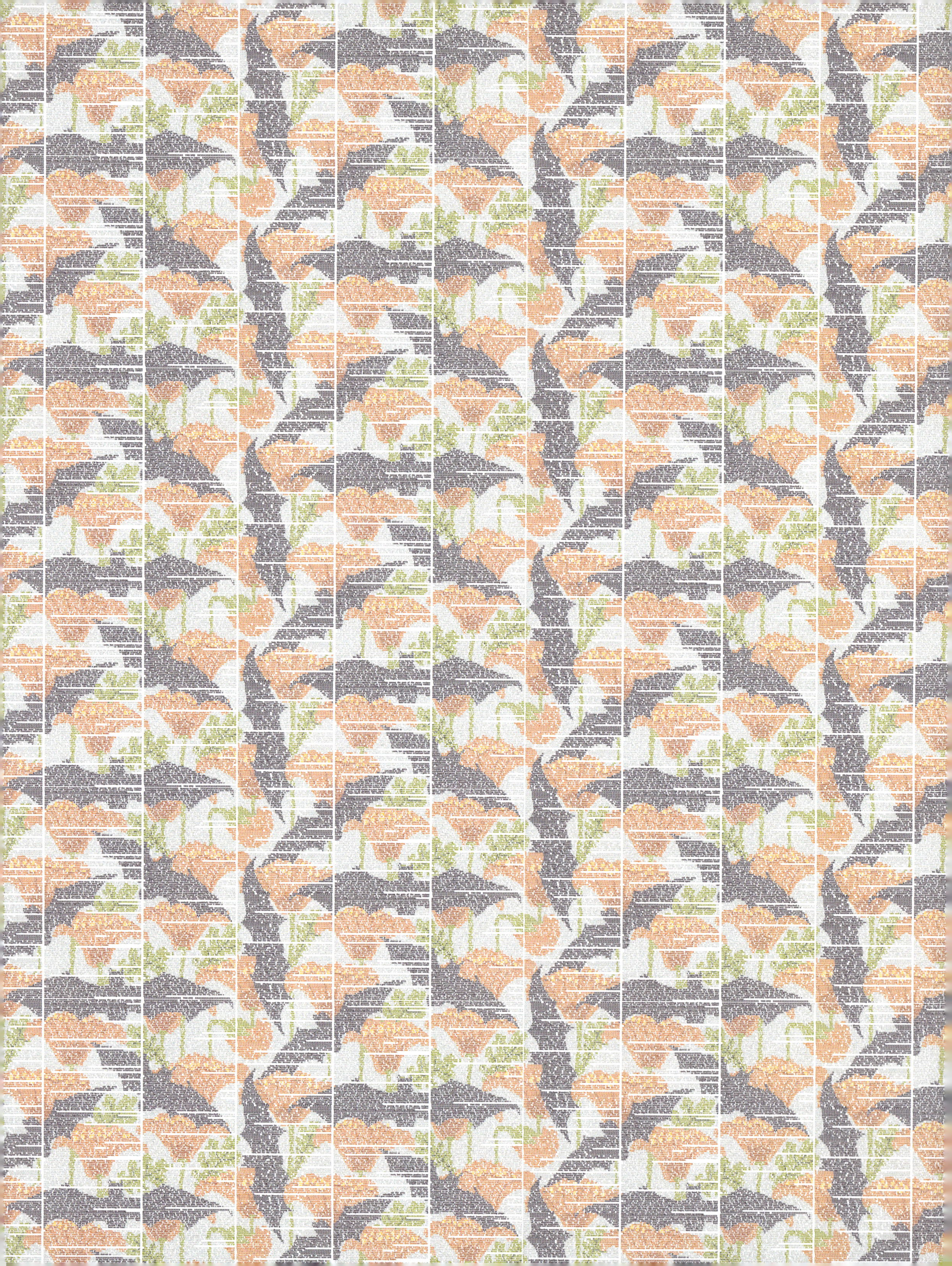

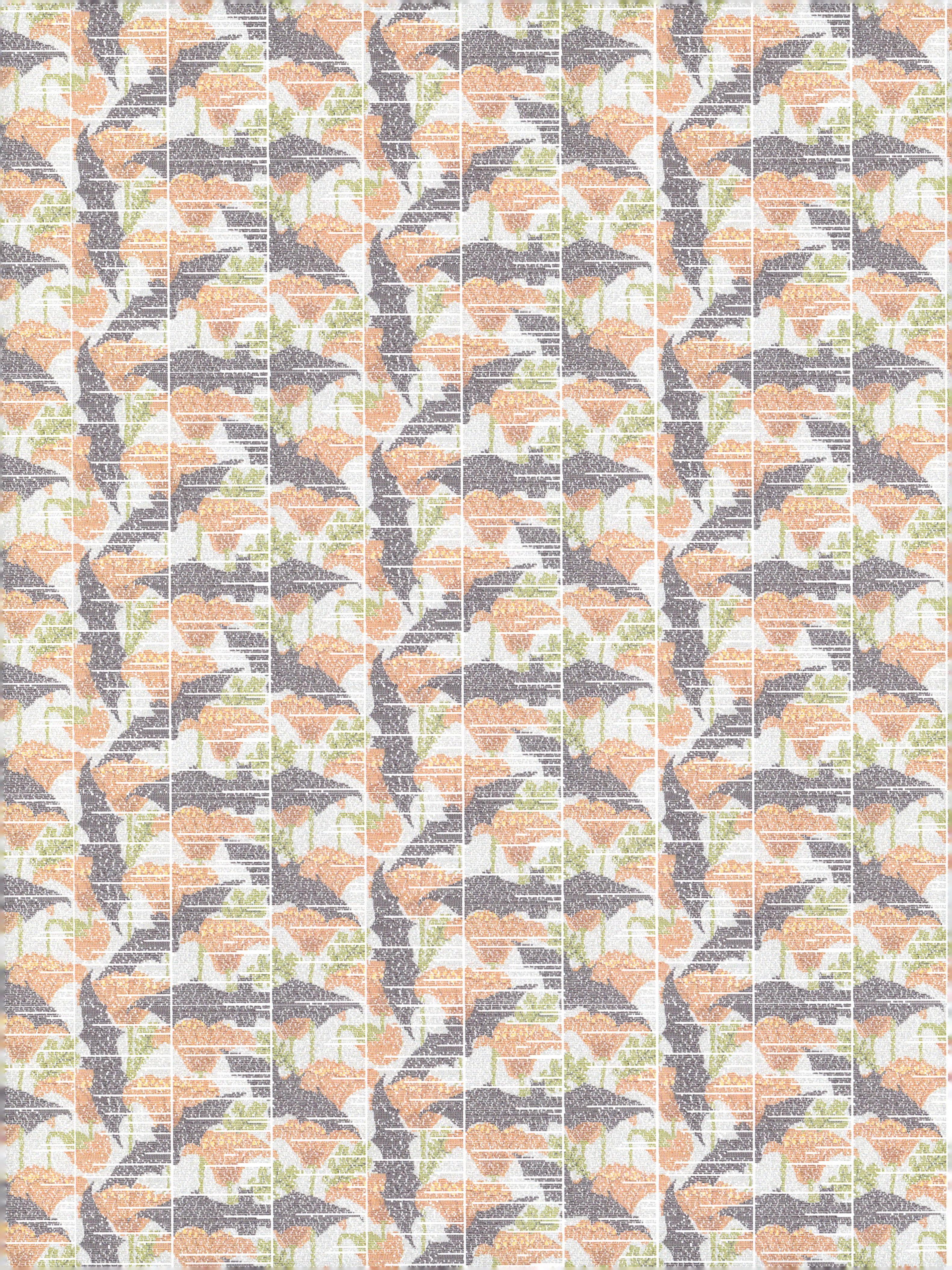

Phylum: Monsters That Cannot Be Seen
Class: Invisible Monsters
Order: Fully and Constantly Invisible

Fully and constantly invisible monsters are the most primitive order of invisible monsters. Hunters, they crave the beefy texture of human flesh, and can devour a coed unnoticed by a slumbering roommate. They kill unceremoniously, gutting the body, though only eating the musculature. This ensures an immediate and silent death as heart, spleen, epidermis and intestine are piled into a sopping mass while limbs and abs become stringy delicacy.

Slights of imagination, overcome by matters of fact. Sustenance seekers; at one with light and dark, occupying only a sliver of space, in which anonymity is achieved through the bending and absorption of light. Mentally registered as tricks or figments, their hungry appraisals of our bodies are felt in random shivers and casual paranoia. Intuited, yet unknowable. There is no protection from these beasts.

Phylum: Monsters That Cannot Be Seen
Class: Invisible Monsters
Order: Selective Invisibility

The predator aesthete selectively controls its appearance by flexing an unimaginable muscle twined through it's skin. A hidden mass of gray-blue-green spreads enzymes that affect visual dissipation. This order of beast prefers partial revelation, existence as a disembodied arm or head floating stiffly against shadow. Carnivorous, sport killers, they thrive on horror, with an equal attraction to shocked paralysis or frenzied bawling. Shock, more than suffering, produces an endorphin that delivers the strained manic sensation of orgasm to the victim and an enhanced flavor to the monster. Their interest is not in the hunt, but for the visual signs accompanying the realization of impending death.

This order divides into families based upon spacial coexistence. The strongest evidence of the demonic is that singular experience of physical and mental spasms that result from mingled corporeality - the disjuncture of human cells as metaphysical matter meshes through. Monsters without co-spacial ability, generally stay in wait, breathing softly in the corner of a room, still, waiting for the full effect of vulnerability, lingering for weeks, even months. Watching their future victim for a moment of self satisfaction or pride, the less apprehension, the better the time to strike.

Phylum: Monsters That Cannot Be Seen
Class: Invisible Monsters
Order: Camouflaged Monsters

Camouflaged mammal derivations adapted within nature. Ostensibly harmless and preferring the solitude of distant caves, forests and waters. Remnants of primitive tribes, abandoned explorers from previous ages, these are human based, highly adapted herbivores, with a plodding gait, who require solitude. Their adaptation generally includes thick, leathery skin identical to the rocks or trees that surround them. These are not hunters, but have highly evolved defense systems, razor sharp, retractable claws up to 6 inches in length. They are highly suspicious and motivated defenders of their territory who will strike with minimal provocation.

Family variants include the ability to control the precise color and texture of the thick epidermis to match immediate surroundings. Genus divisions come along the lines of natural genetic evolution and the chemically manipulated genome derived from scientific experimentation.

Phylum: Monsters That Cannot Be Seen
Class: Invisible Monsters
Order: Unseeable Monsters

Tricksters, masters of hiding; neither invisible nor camouflaged. Unseeable monsters rank among the ugliest. Their visage is startling, and their occasional sightings are responsible for the misconception that monsters represent the social unconscious of physical deformity. Experts at hiding, unseeable monsters are found under beds, in closets, basements, etc. These are not domestic monsters, but also occur in deeply shadowed forests, hiding under water, among the crags of coral, under lilly pads or wrapped in the sea's weeds.

Their skin is sensitive to light, and the 15 watts of a child's nightlight scorches their skin, sparking from the black of shadow, dehydrating their bodies, exasperating their thirst for blood. These hunters prefer small animals and merely nibble at the toes of slumbering humans - same as rats. These monsters thrive disproportionately in paranoid fantasy to the damage they are able to inflict.

They are generally are too well hidden to be seen, but are evidenced by the movement of things they touch, the sounds of their shuffling and the objects they've pilfered. They can flatten themselves to the thickness of paint, weave their bodies into the fabric of silk shirts or fill the crevasse at the bottom of the baseboard. They can transform their scaly shells into the consistency of hair gel, a solid mass of shimmering sludge, smudging itself across the floor.

Phylum: Monsters That Can Be Seen
Class: Bestial Monsters
Order: Fantastical Monsters

These Monsters cannot be described. They bear no concrete relationship to man or any known beast. Their bodies are sustained by an entirely foreign pulminary system, if that's even an appropriate description. They require a chemistry incompatible with our own need for oxygen. They use unknowable forms of locomotion, unfathomed in the darkest tales of witchcraft. They are neither gastropedal nor hovering. They cut through time and space in a manner which bares no corollary. Sensory perception is unique to their form and concepts of sight, touch and taste falter as comparisons. There are no known biological similarities, no possibility of a written analog.

Phylum: Monsters That Can Be Seen
Class: Bestial Monsters
Order: Common Monsters

Chupecabra, werewolves, sea creatures, vampires, Yetti are among the most famous monsters. Fodder for Hollywood grotesquerie, and the staples of cautionary tales and cinema screams.

Ironically, the most famous monsters have become the most endangered. Their weaknesses entered popular culture and inspired centuries of violet daydreaming: monsters can be killed without ethical dilemma. Silver bullets and wooden stakes are known remedies among the smallest children, Saturday morning lore, survival within suburban paranoia. Since the Victorian infatuation with promiscuity and decapitation, the vampire, despite easy reproduction, has become a rarer sight than exotic whales or eagles.

Phylum: Monsters That Can Be Seen
Class: Bestial Monsters
Order: Monsters of the Mist

Electrical storms with consciousness. Gigantic blobs whose true shapes coalesce and dissipate upon the whim of the wind. Generally amorphous, these static charged particles mingle with fog and rain to present a fleeting glimpse of a ferocious countenance hovering above the horizon.

The intentions of mist monsters cannot be definitively discerned; they lack any means of communication. They have neither the means for speech nor a possibility of touch - only a voracious appetite for observation; it is impossible to know what archive these collected observations might feed. As a reader, reclining upon an easy chair in your safest and most familiar surroundings, you are likely in contact with a mist monster. Now; at this very moment.

Contact produces no physical effect, neither gooss-bumped chills, horrified shock nor pressure about the body. Just a flood of paranoia that comes in realizing oneself under constant surveillance. The preparation of your evening meal is carefully observed as well as your most intimate bathroom moments, from simultaneous angles, with both detachment and zeal.

ESCAPE PLAN

Acquisition: It's not stealing if I return it to her purse, if she doesn't notice a thing, if the look in her wallet offers the same view as before. Dusty mints, silver worn from the edges of gum wrappers, that bulging cloth wallet and the greasy dirt imbedded into tapestry flora, matching glasses case trimmed with gold piping, clippers and an emery board scratched irregularly from tumbling among the guts of the purse, various forms of ID and business cards held as a block of worn corners by a cracking rubber band. Using her credit card isn't stealing, because nothing comes up missing.

Winter Coat: Is there a trick to jackets? Are they a perfect apparatus designed to hold in exactly enough heat, and disperse any extra? Would the comfortable jacket I wore in a heated California classroom offer enough protection from the snow? Is the nylon shell and fluffy polyfill gauged with thermostatic accuracy? Is my parka a perpetual heat machine, gathering my 98.6 and holding it in place. If I huddle in a tiny hut along the snowy bank of a distant shore, will my jacket keep me warm? Can my own radiant warmth be harnessed against the effects of a Lake Eerie winter? Or should I dig a hole and live in partially buried hibernation; I don't want to waste my body heat on air contact. There's no buffer in my fight with the cold. Just me and the dirt.

Running away means looking ahead, imagining a new society, so it's the legacy of the Avant Garde. A fast forward to adulthood, dismantling the restrictions of organized play, the structures that keep youth dumb to the possibilities of their own bodies. Running away means envisioning a new symbolic order, wholesale rejection, untwining successive layers of control, fashioning a new epistemology in which the wavering shadows of the forest canopy reveal more than a philosophical musing on Van Gough's shoes. There's no looking back to last year's bright red parka. It's explosion of primary colored stripes doesn't fit the future. I need something earthier, a clearer transition between Chinese factory workmanship and the scarred skins of animals that will eventually warm my body.

Once I've outgrown my city clothes, I'll transform time and nature into an aesthetic of the roughly hewn. Deerskin announces a new personal vision. I'll earn my place slitting the throat of a wide eyed buck, trading stares from bulging eyes, trading his survival for my own. There's no place for polyester, removable sleeves or applique on the banks of Lake Eerie.

Snow Boots: I forget the smudge worn text from the label sewn to the back side of the tongue. It was once a clear indication of size. Maybe the european size remains, or Japanese. But where do I find Asian shoes, those cloth tops with hard plastic soles and a distinct place for the big toe? (It's what ninjas wear.) I'll have to poke a hole in the top of my current pair of tennis shoes, drag my toes through dirt and grass to fray the fresh cut. I can get a replacement for worn out shoes, but not for intentional damage. The cut will have to appear poked through, mesh stretched beyond its breaking point. My mother will complain about the expense, but she expects rough play from her boy, and new shoes are a small price for evidence of masculinity.

It will be difficult to explain my interest in snow boots, but sometimes passion for an object is enough. The quantity of mother's complaints legitimize those occasional indulgences.

We'll go to the department store and I'll stand upon the measure with a salesman bowing before me. I'll make him position it, to feel the charge of his hand wrapping around my foot. Then he'll tickle the slider across arch to ball. I'll learn both length and width, though only one seems to matter.

Guns and Knives: I don't like the immediacy of guns, the now of their action, their place in the trajectory of industrial progress, their remove from the intensity of the kill. Mechanical dehumanization, for both the gunman and the prey. It's a sculpture of coercion wielded with a false sense of power embodied in cinematic standoff, that circle jerk of anxiety: a group of men, each with a gun trained upon him, none with the guts to shoot.

In a new society, equality matters most. I'll have to take down a grizzly with my bear hands. It's fair if I hop on it's matted fur back, grab stiff bristled patches to hold my place on the ferocious ride. Against the bucking of his enormous trunk, I'll climb the bear like he climbs a tree, racing for life itself. I can muster the strength to crack its neck, so that he collapses under me, falls as a fleshy trembling lump, convulsions suppressed by his own heft. Powerful jaws become a cave of drool. And then, I'll need a knife to excavate the body, find the usable parts, the tastiest muscles, separate skin from bone. Something large, a blade that could double as a saw, hack the girth of a small tree and carve the bone of a large bear. An all purpose blade, something with a hand guard - safety against resistance. Single edged. Serrated - the thick, dense mass of a femur is not a score and snap proposition.

Matches: Rubbing sticks together is tiring and doesn't always work.

Rope: A supine lasso to snare a hare. Booby traps: a construction capable of releasing an enormous rolling boulder, or sending the sharpened stumps of trees skewering an interloping body. My new society will realize the spirit of hollywood myth, inflated in the stagnate cycling of suburban fantasy.

Plane or Bus Ticket: In running away, how important is speed? Is the circuitous route of a bus line an adequate foil? Disperate sightings couldn't betray my ultimate goal. I would navigate up through the fields and falls of Boise, then down to the deserted planes of Lubbock. Tracing north over the ghosts of Oklahoma to the rocky landscape of the Dakota's. I'll lose myself among Chicago smoke and brick before crossing the flatlands and steel plants of Indiana. I'll have time to tour towns listed in the return addresses of junk mail: Terre Haute, Fort Wayne. The northern cities of Ohio would present a predictable path, so I'll backtrack along the Mississippi, like Huck Finn then maneuver Appalachia, making my final push north through West Virginia.

On a plane, I might travel thousands of miles in a day, only to have police waiting for my arrival at the end of registered travel. I'd make it to the frontier only to be captured like a dog, shipped back in a plastic and wire crate.

I had that familiar pain of hesitation in my gut before I even reached the corner. Another practice run; testing how far I could get before anxiety took control. My fear of the world, that wide blue horizon, competing versions of American accents, and unfamiliar labels on soda pop cans. The totality of the unknown was an empty slate of transitory morals, but without the meager safety net of scheduled meals provided at the family home.

It just wasn't time to leave.

I walked in the deep ditch, looking for coke bottles, jumping up to cross the points where gravel and culvert pipe allowed automotive access. I kept a lookout for the sparkle of glass; each bottle puts another dime toward my operation. It was only three doors down, the tiny yellow house that seemed more dusty than derelict. Its pieces were intact: faded wood doors, charcoal roof and sliding windows with torn and frayed, corroded metal screens, but it had an aura of abandonment. The only sign of life was a mongrel tied to a tree by a scruffy line of chain and nylon rope. He was a muscular mutt with a black monochrome of zebra stripes across his trunk, short, thick drooling muzzle and floppy velvet ears. He barked vigorously as I passed, though it wasn't personal. I might as well have been a noise on the wind. The neglected animal only raged against circumstance, the futility of an inner life, the desire for an impossible violence.

I felt envy, stepped closer to see the inflamed pink receding into nostrils and bloating from around swollen eyes. His ears tucked back, and his thick jowls revealed black spotted gums. As if by static charge, patches of wiry hair rose upon his back, while his tail curled between his legs, wound tight to the undercarriage, pressed hard against his own balls.

I tucked my fingers against my palm and offered a sniff of my hand, hoping he'd recognize our common bond and that we would find mutual serenity in the kindness of my gesture. But the growl intensified; the chain strained a deep line of pressure around the front of his neck. He pulled himself onto hind legs

and kicked furiously against the dirt, trying desperately to maintain his new height, to challenge me on bipedal terms.

I moved my hand toward his nose, maintaining an inch of distance. The dog's fury increased as I drew closer. He circled with a snarl, and ended the retreat in a lunge that caught the chain in mid air, jerking the mongrel into a sideways slide across his dirty rut. We were each lost in our own fantasies of wide horizons, American accents and soda pop cans. I needed this dog, this mutt, mongrel, to know our similarities, the shared totality of our latent violence. I offered him the tip of my finger, knowing he would understand the salty metallic taste on his tiny front teeth.

Reasons to Leave

Something about the possibility of air, the challenge wind makes to a tree. The losing proposition of rattling branches and a disembodied moan. Hickory trees are the dream of the east, something deciduous, foreign, but with a familiar phonic resemblance to "Ichabod." HIK·OR·E. IK·A·BOD. It's a world of winter terror in which trees stripped bare slash the sky. The sun is the only remaining trace of life, that light at the end of the tunnel. The great gray of its bark, the violent monochrome of night, its emptiness both proof and texture of the demonic. A moonlit, paranoid fury - still, silent and glaring. The aural similarity to a character in an outdated horror story is enough to inspire damage. This is why I chose Lake Eerie. The name alone makes the town a primary site of adolescent male freedom fantasy. Running into the forest, raging over the rustle of leaves, unfazed by the snap and cut of passing branches. Eerie is named for its preponderance of Indian cemeteries, sites of satanic ritual, for the parts of the forest that defy physics and the howling that cuts the crisp stillness of Spring. Eerie doesn't exist on any mortal coil, it's a dot on a map dotted by factories, a Motel 6, cabin and boat rentals with botched signage, fishing shacks and cozy diners. But there is an existential overlay, a space only seen by aspiring adventurers during grade school geography lessons. Its a name that captures the imagination and holds it hostage to the darkest wonderment of terrified youth.

Drifter Aesthetics

Hitching an oblique course on the charm of my smile and the innocence of my eyes. I'm the aesthete, scanning the roadway for signs of...

The wrinkled pucker of a toothless mouth stares out from the cab of a dilapidated pick-up on a highway through the Ozarks. Armadillo tails never seem to rot. Hills as green as postcards of Ireland. A flowing scrap of a plastic sheet, hooked on bramble, glanced in passing under the distant light of a streetlamp becomes St Christopher. That hunched traveler, supported by a staff, shrouded in muslin. The distinct lines of farmland growing plants I can't identify. I overheard, "There were all these pedals and a keyhole." Sticks of shrubbery, browned grasses, lesions of red clay. The dismembered head of a sparrow. Once glassy eyes, now errant scabs in the soft order of plumage. Past the rugged remains of a neckline, rigid strings dried around a brown chunk of spine. The furry, skeletal remains of a chipmunk wearing a glass suit papered by the metallic gold of a Miller label - still attached to a curved shard of an erstwhile bottle. The yellowed ring of a condom, cracking nearby. A red 1980's Chevy Citation with a white hood. Pink bondo fender, grey primer door. Muddy lace panties. A stiffened brown bundle among dried yellow weeds, surrounded by foxtails and rabbit shit. Plastic bags caught in trees during a recent windstorm. Grocery store flags, empty, waving futilely, knowing they've already carried their weight. The ruins of roadside amusements. Splintered grey plywood, faded and peeling paint, rusted remains of mechanical supports, every bit as exotic as pyramids or Parthenon. A cardboard box labeled with thick black marker: ApoCALyPse.

Utopia

The end of the world is a purely visual event; it's intellectual legacy, the redefinition of significant form. Every smear, crack, puddle, clod, chip or shard is part of the same monochrome of existence, each just as charged as any other. Grayness fused to insignificance, rubble is the greatest technological possibility. The coveted landscape of Abercrombie abs, sublime awe smoothed into deep cuts by the force of nature, harnessed on an Ab Rocket. But rigor mortis makes that taught musculature uncomfortably bumpy, harsh, less washboard and more cheese grater. The radiant warmth of suntanned perfection converts to the fractured pattern of a dried lake bed, flaking into jagged polygons. Sexy chaos among the the fissured sheen of glass.

Desire becomes complete in the strip-down experience of aesthetic collapse. Wants are dislodged from expectation, squarely fused to texture and hue. The last man on earth isn't preserving conventions, choosing social bodies. Rather, he's an aesthete immersed in pleasant sensations, hunting for softness among the rubble.

The missing limbs of a beautiful stranger reveal personal agency as pathetic excess, a smudge of an erstwhile life. The final act of the most alluring post apocalyptic biceps was to pull the weight of his lacerated body through its own blood. Smearing: the final creative act, some ultimate expressionist gesture of streaks and pools. As his open wounds slid against the floor, he focused on the future through shrieking sobs. Velour print upholstery was never the best idea. Nearing death, he never considered his own insignificance against meteoric shrapnel, flesh eating plague, nuclear radiation or terrorist what-have-you.

Tastefully draped and perfectly soaked. Jeans, exquisitely bleached and frayed in a third world sweatshop to signify waspish rapacity, now cover a mess of separating sores too coagulated to comfortably slide ones body against.

Sweetness becomes the primary concern in a post apocalyptic necrology. Sky blue desiccated eyes, hollow in their longing, loose in their sockets, but good enough for a hard-on. He's beautiful until his skin turns that particular shade of corpse black and his belly opens up to lesions and larvae, white worms muddling through a mass of pinkish fat. His ass is a different kind of breeding ground, no longer the worst smelling part of his body. And when I kiss his mouth I hear him speak through me, like reading words in a dream, their idea comes across through mystical anonymity. The secrets his body reveals can only be translated through the random banging of typewriter keys.

Perfect bodies can't be preserved. I'd never pick a pocket to find an ID and determine some actual name. I like "Timmy," Lassie's companion in innocent kindness. "Timmy" is comfortable with the nonverbal; he understands Lassie's subjective combination of scratching and tugging, canid reports that youthful indiscretions lead a pair of small children down an abandoned well. And in the deep alone of that great black pit, they might submit to temptations equally dark. I feel love for the first time, ascribing sweetness to the dusty awkwardness of "Timmy's" broken body. It's an intense feeling, something I never knew alive, but read all through his decay. There's no illusion of forever; "Timmy" is closer to dust than reciprocity.

Love handles have the stiff malleability of clay, preserving the shape of my grip along loosely defined hips. Blood clots about the eyes and nostrils are imperfections that can be overlooked. Damage from the scruff of my own face is another story. Kissing can't become biting and chin-stubble could scratch its way down to something disturbing. Kissing through a plastic bag, hole torn to accommodate my tongue. There's no suffocation hazard, but no intimacy either. He functions at my whim, and that's the entirety of attraction. "Timmy" never complains; he understands the impending abandonment. He knows that despite everything we've shared, I have to walk away without him. My back won't sustain his weight and his limbs wouldn't withstand the strain.

It can't be rape without protest so it's making love: physical, pure, actual. "Timmy's" last moments as solid mass are devoted to me. His compound fractures approximate recent changes in architectural style; trendy to death. When the sexiest bodies resemble an accidental cave within the rubble of a collapsed building, is it wrong to want to be inside? Vultures prefer the soft hairs at the base of the belly, while insects enjoy the challenge of mamilla. Electricity is gone, so refrigeration is no savior. Sunlight and soldier flies are the great enemies of lasting happiness.

I don't know how I ended up as the last one, how I survived the plague, choking dust, lack of sunlight, watermarks, rot of flood, glowing radiation or lab-created virus. I am the last man on earth; biological success. Fucking the miscellaneous remains of random bodies should be beneath me. If I'm the chosen one, why is this my choice?

If I dropped a mess of an aesthetic masterpiece from the strapped seat of an overturned Honda, dragged his randomized lump over shattered sheets of safety glass, gouging bloodless wounds across his back, would it be a rescue? Would I be entitled to exact a price on the remains of that body, indulge myself as the justified payment for my assistance, or has the forfeiture of his life made him public domain, property for the taking, something to claim with the planting of a flag. An apocalyptic Misery, though Kathy Bates was wrong, and I'm alright. Remember, my captives make no protest. He's mine, fair and square. All that's left of humanity is what's left in my head. Finders keepers. Possession is nine tenths of what's left of the law. A landscape of raw exploits and morality fabricated on the fly, It's a new society that will last until it rots.

With the exception of c[illegible] vertically, blowing a charred [illegible] sagging shingle and leaving unscathed, it was difficult to te[illegible] been abandoned. There was a p[illegible] of disrepair or disassemble. A m[illegible] mean empty, just broken. Broken [illegible] peeling veneer revealing the skelet[illegible] core. Several families might live be[illegible] protected only by an aluminum m[illegible] entrance. Their pooled resources fe[illegible] naked children, covered a miniscule mort[illegible] against the home, that meager inheritanc[illegible] and speed don't come cheap.

Discerning decrepit from abandoned is a[illegible] of connoisseurship. After people leave, the[illegible] are the first to go. Kids don't start the destru[illegible] they finish it. Kids don't understand that a house [illegible] copper mine, and the junk of its guts gets traded [illegible] cash.

After pans and clothes are packed into the be[illegible] of an El Camino, under flashlight and moonlight, the house is open to all. The neighbors' friendly waving hands become the desperado's violent grasp: punching through plaster, pulling out wire. Wad it up, burn it up. The plastic housing melts away leaving pure salvage value in its place. Maybe 80 cents a pound.

Toilets, swag lamps, faucets and drawer pulls are currency, replacements for something broken, saved for a special occasion. Poverty is navigated with a stockpile of porcelain and pull-chains. Potential use, potential value, trash to trade in a time of need.

When kids come, windows break. It's an introduction to transgression, breaking a familial structure from a safe distance. The duration of a rock's flight through space allows plausible deniability, the warped reflection of total destruction.

Graffiti inscribes new values: loves and hates, cunts and fucks, lyrics for feelings, gypsum dust scraped into lines.

Bodies replace Barbies. Square haircuts and ink pen makeovers become the taste of tongue and sweat, the smells of crotch and jerky breath. Coke cans become beer cans, black label bottles among cigarette butts. Practicing addiction is a private affair; its public premier must be convincing. Growing up means learning tolerance, but still, no niggers allowed.

Front yards were junkyards and back yards were worse. The front yard held forgotten fruit trees, planted for sustenance by a depression era mother. Most remained small, withered. Only one was suitable for climbing. Debris piled around trees, the strewn remains of home improvement. A rusty lawnmower, poised to tackle the weeds that grew up through its wheels. A useless red wagon, leaning at one corner, its red body rinsed with rust. The metal became a jagged filigree mapping an

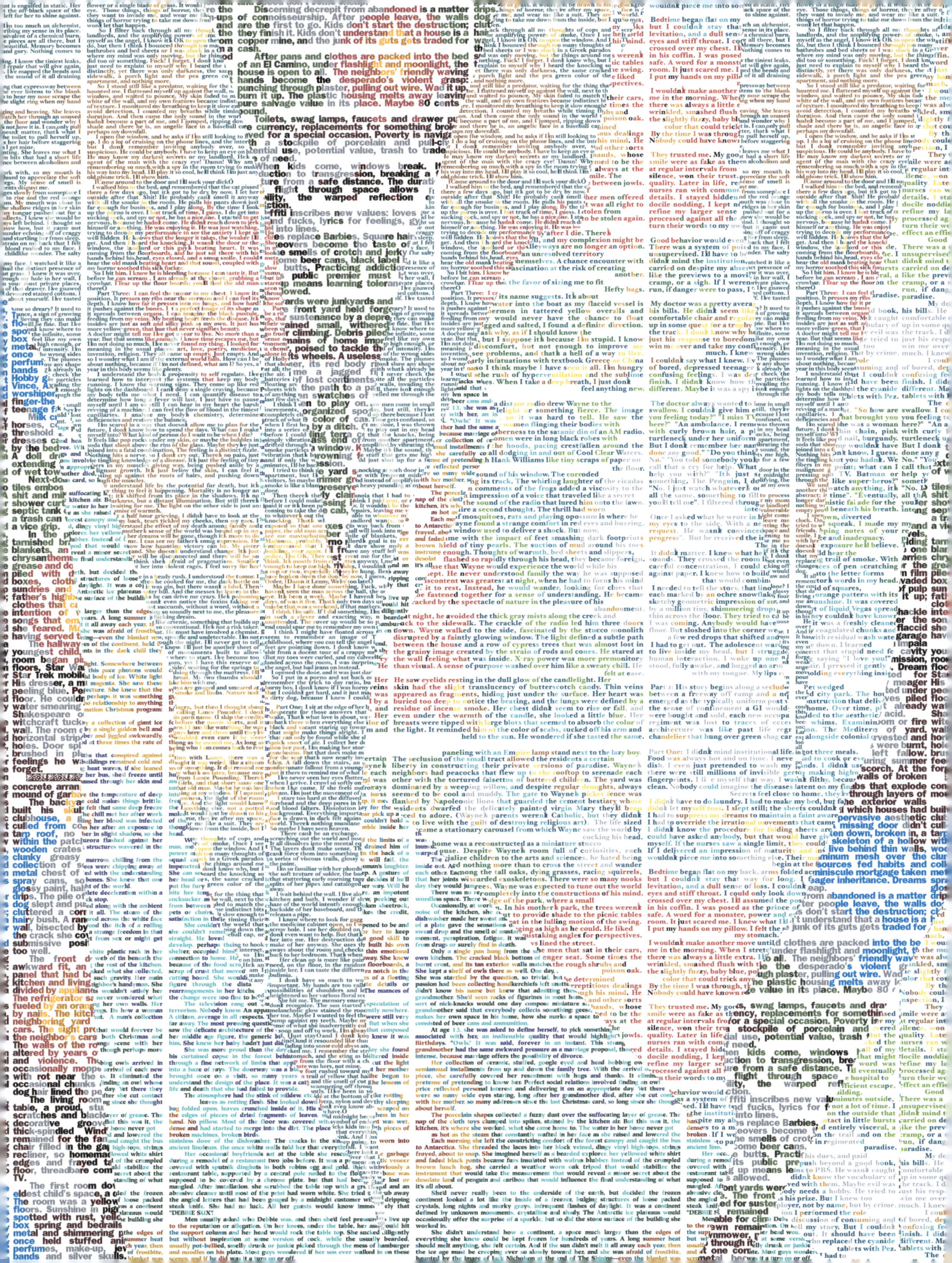

Discerning decrepit from abandoned is a matter of connoisseurship. After people leave, the walls are the first to go. Kids don't start the destruction; they finish it. Kids don't understand that a house is a copper mine, and the junk of its guts gets traded for cash.

After pans and clothes are packed into the bed of an El Camino, under flashlight and moonlight, the house is open to all. The neighbors' friendly waving hands become the desperado's violent grasp: punching through plaster, pulling out wire. Wad it up, burn it up. The plastic housing melts away leaving pure salvage value in its place. Maybe 80 cents pound.

Toilets, swag lamps, faucets and drawer pu[lls] re currency, replacements for something brok[en] ved for a special occasion. Poverty is naviga[ted] th a stockpile of porcelain and pull-ch[ains] ential use, potential value, trash to trade of need.

When kids come, windows break. I[ntro]duction to transgression, breaking a [pic]ture from a safe distance. The durati[on of] flight through space allows [poss]ibility, the warped reflection [of] ction.

[Gra]ffiti inscribes new values: loves [a]nd fucks, lyrics for feelings, gy[...] into lines.

[...]es replace Barbies. Square hair [...]eovers become the taste of [th]e smells of crotch and jerky [...]ome beer cans, black label [...] butts. Practicing addictio[n...] public premier must [...] up means learning toleran[ce...] lowed.

[...]ards were junkyards and [...] front yard held forg[...] sustenance by a depre[...] ained small, withered [...] climbing. Debris piled [...] mains of home impr[ovement], poised to tackle th[...] its wheels. A useless [...] er, its red body ri[...]

www.ingramcontent.com/pod-product-compliance
Lightning Source LLC
LaVergne TN
LVHW071632100826
845154LV00008BA/137
9780981462370